Start Your Own Sole Proprietorship

by

Kim Isaac Greenblatt, EA

Kim Greenblatt Publisher
Published In West Hills, California
United States of America

Start Your Own Sole Proprietorship, Start Your Own Sole Proprietorship
by Kim Isaac Greenblatt, EA

Disclosure: The advice given in this book is current to the best of the author's knowledge as of the time of the publishing of this book. Please exercise due diligence, research and common sense in starting your own business. Good luck!

Published by Kim Greenblatt,
West Hills, California, United States of America.

ISBN-13 978-1-60622-006-1

Library of Congress Control Number: 2011906440

June 2011

Dedicated to People Who Are Looking To Become Masters of their Own Fate, Captains of their Own Ships, or At Least Make Enough Money to Pay the Bills

TABLE OF CONTENTS

Introduction

Welcome! If you are reading this book you want to start your own business. If you are like a lot of us in this current economic environment you may be reinventing yourself, may have decided that you want to do something that you love for a living or maybe you have to get an income stream going. Maybe you are coming out of college and are excited and ready to launch your own business. Let me see if I can get you on a path to try to help you materialize your dreams.

My name is Kim Isaac Greenblatt. I am a businessman. I have had a lot of businesses in my life and have had success (and failure) with each of them. I am also a tax preparer and an Enrolled Agent (that is what the initials "EA" mean after my last name). An enrolled agent is a person who has earned the privilege of practicing that is, representing taxpayers, before the Internal Revenue Service. Enrolled agents, like attorneys and certified public accountants (CPAs), are unrestricted as to which taxpayers they can represent, what types of tax matters they can handle, and which IRS offices they can practice before.
My perspective is a unique one because I have seen a lot of people who have had great business plans, great businesses and did not plan for tax implications. You, having the great sense to read this book, will be light years ahead of the others and know what is out there for you.

So what are you up against? Besides taking into consideration income taxes, you should be aware that you are up against a world economy again and depending on what you are trying to do, you may be going against manufacturing from all over the world. You may have your ideas stolen within weeks of being on the market. Can you live with that? If you are thinking of trying to start a business outside of the United States don't kid yourself. You will often pay more in taxes offshore and sometimes that will be in the form of bribes or under the table payments. There is no free lunch anywhere you go on the planet these days. The United States still has the capacity and ability to be one of the greatest places on earth despite what the media and pundits are trying to tell us.

Part of the reason is people like you! You rock!

That being said, if you have the ability to come up with a great concept for yourself and the drive to materialize it the chances are that you will do and find a way to overcome whatever obstacles are presented in your way. You just have to find your niche. Hopefully this book can at least give you at least one great idea that you can use.
If you are on the fence for starting your own business this book should push you in one direction or another. Being your own boss means taking responsibility for things that an employer would in the past. The way that the corporate environment is changing these days you may not be missing much by going into business for yourself. If you like being master (or mistress) of your own destiny then you may want to consider starting your own gig.

If after reading this book you decide that it is too much aggravation that works too. Pat yourself on the back because you may have saved yourself thousands of dollars in money that you might have lost trying to run a business that you will discover that you didn't like.

This book also is about starting a sole proprietorship. Ah, and what is that?

A *sole proprietorship* is a type of business entity. It is one of many types of business entities here in the United States of America. The others are partnerships, corporations, limited liability partnerships, and limited liability companies. They will not be covered in this book. Just getting to the sole proprietorship will be plenty for now. Each entity type has very specific rules and tax instructions by laws on how the

business is conducted and how it reports income and pays taxes. It also may vary from state to state.
A sole proprietorship is not as structured as some of the other entities, which must have documents governing operations and must be registered with the state before beginning business and which only go out of business when legally dissolved. That can be a real problem which we will talk about later. A sole proprietorship exists whenever a person decides to engage in a business activity for profit and ends whenever the person no longer engages in the activity for profit.

Sole proprietorships are operated by the business person alone without any partners. Unlike corporations, limited liability partnerships, and limited liability companies, the business has no separate legal existence from its owner. So, you, the lucky business owner, are personally liable for all debts and judgments against the proprietorship.
Unlike partnerships and corporations, which report income and expenses on a separate tax form (out of scope for this book), a sole proprietor reports their business income and expenses on Schedule C, and the net profit or loss transfers to their Form 1040. Those are Federal tax forms and you might have requirements for reporting depending on what state you live in. Let's get rolling with starting your own sole proprietorship.

Kim Isaac Greenblatt
April 24 2011

What are the types of business entities?

Of all the choices you make when starting a business, one of the most important is the type of legal organization you select for your company. This decision can affect how much you pay in taxes, the amount of paperwork your business is required to do, the personal liability you face and your ability to borrow money. Business formation is controlled by the law of the state where your business is organized.

The most common forms of businesses are:

Sole Proprietorships
Partnerships
Corporations
Limited Liability Companies (LLC)
While state law controls the formation of your business, federal tax law controls how your business is taxed. Federal tax law recognizes an additional business form, the Subchapter S Corporation.

All businesses must file an annual return. The form you use depends on how your business is organized. Sole proprietorships and corporations file an income tax return. Partnerships and S Corporations file an information return. For an LLC with at least two members, except for some businesses that are automatically classified as a corporation, it can choose to be classified for tax purposes as either a corporation or a partnership. A business with a single member can choose to be classified as either a corporation or disregarded as an entity separate from its owner, that is, a "disregarded entity."

As a disregarded entity the LLC will not file a separate return instead all the income or loss is reported by the single member/owner on its annual return.

The answer to the question "What structure makes the most sense?" depends on the individual circumstances of each business owner. Most people start in an entity way beyond what they need and that includes disregarded entities. People complain because in some states, like California, as a corporation at the state level, you are on the hook for $800 a year whether you made money or not. If you start up your business late in a year, say Nov 2011, you are on the hook for 2011 and 2012 taxes so $800 x 2 = $1600. Major yikes!

If you need to have a partnership or corporation because of the business you are in, that is great, however this book may not be for you.

The type of business entity you choose will depend on:

Liability
Taxation
Recordkeeping
Sole Proprietorship

A sole proprietorship is the most common form of business organization. It's easy to form and offers complete control to the owner. It is any unincorporated business owned entirely by one individual. In general, the owner is also personally liable for all financial obligations and debts of the business. (State law may also govern this area depending on the state.)

Sole proprietors can operate any kind of business. It must be a business, not an investment or hobby. It can be full-time or part-time work. This includes operating a:

Shop or retail trade business
Large company with employees
Home based business
One person consulting firm
Every sole proprietor is required to keep sufficient records to comply with federal tax requirements regarding business records.

Generally, sole proprietors file Schedule C or C-EZ, Profit or Loss from Business, with their Form 1040. Sole proprietor farmers file Schedule F, Profit or Loss from Farming. Your net business income or loss is combined with your other income and deductions and taxed at individual rates on your personal tax return.

Sole proprietors must also pay self-employment tax on the net income reported on Schedule C or Schedule F. You may also be able to deduct one-half of SE tax on your 1040. Use Schedule SE, Self-Employment Tax, to compute this tax.

Sole proprietors do not have taxes withheld from their business income so you will generally need to make quarterly estimated tax payments if you expect to make a profit. These estimated payments include both income tax and self-employment taxes for Social Security and Medicare.

Partnership

A partnership is the relationship existing between two or more persons who join to carry on a trade or business. Each person contributes money, property, labor or skill, and expects to share in the profits and losses of the business.

A partnership does not pay any income tax at the partnership level. Partnerships file Form 1065, U.S. Return of Partnership Income, to report income and expenses. This is an information return. The partnership passes the information to the individual partners on Schedule K-1, Partner's Share of Income, Credits, and Deductions. Partnerships are often referred to as pass-through or flow-through entities for this reason.

Each partner reports his share of the partnership net profit or loss on his personal Form 1040 tax return. Partners must report their share of partnership income even if a distribution is not made.

Partners are not employees of the partnership and so taxes are not withheld from any distributions. Like sole proprietors, partners generally need to make quarterly estimated tax payments if they expect to make a profit.

General partners must pay self-employment tax on their net earnings from self employment assigned to them from the partnership. Net earnings from self- employment include an individual's share, distributed or not, of income or loss from any trade or business carried on by a partnership.

Limited partners are subject to self-employment tax only on guaranteed payments, such as professional fees for services rendered.

Corporation

A corporate structure is more complex than other business structures. It requires complying with more regulations and tax requirements. It may require more tax preparation services than the sole proprietorship or the partnership.

Corporations are formed under the laws of each state and are subject to corporate income tax at the federal and generally at the state level. In addition, any earnings distributed to shareholders in the form of dividends are taxed at individual tax rates on their personal tax returns.

The corporation is an entity that handles the responsibilities of the business. Like a person, the corporation can be taxed and can be held legally liable for its actions. If you organize your business as a corporation, you are generally not personally liable for the debts of the corporation. (Exceptions may exist under state law.)

When you form a corporation, you create a separate tax-paying entity. Unlike sole proprietors and partnerships, income earned by a corporation is taxed at the corporate level using corporate tax rates. Regular corporations are called C corporations because Subchapter C of Chapter 1 of the Internal Revenue Code is where you find general tax rules affecting corporations and their shareholders.

A corporation files Form 1120 or 1120-A, U.S. Corporation Income Tax Return. If a shareholder is an employee, he pays income tax on his wages, and the corporation and the employee each pay one half of the social security and Medicare taxes and the corporation can deduct its half. A corporate shareholder pays only income tax for any dividends received, which may be subject to a dividends-received deduction.

Subchapter S Corporation

The Subchapter S Corporation is a variation of the standard corporation. The S corporation allows income or losses to be passed through to individual tax returns, similar to a partnership. The rules for Subchapter S corporations are found in Subchapter S of Chapter 1 of the Internal Revenue Code.

An S corporation has the same corporate structure as a standard corporation. It is a legal entity, chartered under state law, and is separate from its shareholders and officers. There is generally limited liability for corporate shareholders. The difference is that the corporation files an election on Form 2553, Election by a Small Business Corporation, to be treated differently for federal tax purposes.

Generally, an S corporation is exempt from federal income tax other than tax on certain capital gains and passive income. It is treated in the same way as a partnership, in that generally taxes are not paid at the corporate level.

An S corporation files Form 1120S, U.S. Corporation Income Tax Return for an S Corporation. The income flows through to be reported on the shareholders' individual returns. Schedule K-1, Shareholder's Share of Income, Credits and Deductions, is completed with Form 1120S for each shareholder. The Schedule K-1 tells shareholders their allocable share of corporate income and deductions. Shareholders must pay tax on their share of corporate income, regardless of whether it is actually distributed.

Limited Liability Company

A Limited Liability Company (LLC) is a relatively new business structure allowed by state statute.

LLCs are popular because, similar to a corporation, owners generally have limited personal liability for the debts and actions of the LLC. Other features of LLCs are more like a partnership, providing management flexibility and the benefit of pass-through taxation. Owners of an LLC are called members. Since most states do not restrict ownership, members may include individuals, corporations, other LLCs and foreign entities. Most states also permit "single member" LLCs, those having only one owner.

A few types of businesses generally cannot be LLCs, such as banks and insurance companies. Check your state's requirements and the federal tax regulations for further information. There are special rules for foreign LLCs.

For additional information on the kinds of tax returns to file, how to handle employment taxes and possible pitfalls, refer to Publication 3402, Tax Issues for Limited Liability Companies.

Which structure best suits your business?

One form is not necessarily better than any other. Each business owner must assess his or her own needs. It may be important to seek advice from business experts and professionals when considering the advantages and disadvantages of a business entity. For the purposes of our book, I want to suggest that you start off as a Sole Proprietorship.

No Money, Need To Work, No Time For Business Yet

If you are in a position where you are debt, either out of work or under-employed, you need to get another income stream. The facts are that you don't have income to start a second job. You are not in a position other than to work for somebody else.

If you can, try and get an internship in the field you want to work in and try to get a small salary or any kind of money to establish legitimacy in the business.

If you end up working for somebody else, start saving your money or use it to draw down the debts that are keeping you from going after what you really want in life.

Set a realistic plan to pay off any debts you have and make up your mind to get it done. It will happen.

Banks should be loaning money and as you may have discovered that they are pretty tight with their cash after being bailed out. You may have been in a position to access money from the bank and that money is cut off.

This will be a good time to cut costs, if you can. Start looking around your neighborhood, on the Internet, asking friends what is out there that you might be able to do to make some extra money.

This isn't the time to be bashful.

There are a lot of other people out of work and at least for the interim, it is going to get worse before it gets better. The people who will make it through this will have discipline and will be able to stay solvent.

I have faith in you. If you try, it may not be easy, but you will be able to do it!

Things You Should Consider When Picking A Business

One of the biggest questions I get asked is, "Kim, what kind of business should I get into? What is the next 'big thing'?"

If I could predict the next big thing I wouldn't be consulting, doing taxes, writing, publishing, managing or coding. I would be doing the next 'big thing'.

The cliché answer is unless you really have an innate ability for correctly guessing the fickle public's taste; don't bother trying to guess what the public wants next unless you have a lot of money to burn. The number one thing you should be looking at is whether or not you like the business you want to get into. It is a lot easier to do something you love than something you hate. Millions of people around the world are doing jobs just to get by. Here is a chance to do the one thing that you love.

You like to design rooms? If you think you can make a living with it in the market you are in, go for it. Bear in mind that you will have to figure out a business plan before you can actually start your business but make sure it is something that you love doing.

You may be pleasantly surprised that your business may turn into the next "big thing" and you will be there waiting to take advantage of it. The number two thing you should consider is what is your realistic income potential?

You may like to design rooms but if everybody else in Trenton, New Jersey or Ankara, Turkey is also interested in designing rooms the chances are that you will have a lot of people offering to design rooms for free. You will have a hard time paying the bills. Keep in mind that jobs (full or part-time) that are glamorous, exciting or fun have a lot of people wanting to do them. Competition is fierce and the market reflects the income you can potentially make accordingly.

If you are starting something brand new, or something yucky (cleaning out people's sewer lines), you will have less people (depending on the market in your area) in competition so you can forecast a better income stream.

Whatever it is that you decide to do, take the time to make a business plan. A business plan is a blueprint for what you are planning to do. It should serve as a written document you can show others, potential bankers or people with money to invest (if you go that route) that you know what you are doing and know the direction that you will be going towards.

Let's say that you've decided to do the job of your dreams. You really enjoy baking things at home. You think you would make a great baker. Maybe you love to fix things around the house. You've sat down and you have worked out that you think you could make a pretty good living doing this. The next question you need to ask yourself is, "How easy is it for me to get started in the business?" This is called the ease of entry into the business or initial starting requirements.

You need to know or be able to research what the requirements are for doing business in the particular field that you want to work in. A good place to start is to strike up conversations with people who are doing what you are doing and don't live near your geographical location. If you want to be a plumber, for example, you may want to talk to one that isn't close to you so the person won't feel threatened. In the case of being a plumber, he (or she) probably won't feel threatened because there is a specific path of entry into being a plumber - you need to apprentice with an experienced plumber, take classes, etc.

This is the type of information you need to figure out before getting into your business. Do you have to have any specific licensing requirements for the city, county, state or national level in order to demonstrate competency for what you are planning on doing? You don't want a doctor who has had one year of junior college making a diagnosis on you and it is to be expected that different careers or businesses have different requirements.

If you don't have the requirements now, your mission is to determine what do you need to do to get the skills, how long will it take and will it be worth my while to go through the process to learn the skill or trade or get the street credentials that you might need.

That dovetails nicely into the next factor for consideration:

Is there a market demand for what you want to do?

You very well may want to be a plumber but if there are already ten plumbers in your area and there aren't a lot of people, there may not be a lot of work to go around. On the other hand in a large city like New York, Los Angeles, Chicago, Houston or Miami, you may not have to worry about finding work since there are enough people with broken sinks, toilets and water pipes to go around.

Here is where you take stock of your existing skill sets. If you have always been handy since you were a kid and have read up on how to change pipes, love working with PVC, and already have connections in the industry - you are on your way. The remaining aspect to this would be to demonstrate reliable work habits - are you on time for your jobs, are you honest, do you go the extra mile for your customers, things like that.

If on the other hand you hate working with your hands, hate getting dirty and have a fear of dirty water, maybe plumbing isn't the career choice for you.

You've found a great job you want to do, you have the knowledge that you can make a living at the job, and there is demand for your skills.

But is your job recession proof?

Are you doing something that withstand the swings that we sometimes encounter (like now for argument's sake) when people's checkbooks close and money is tight? Is the job or product or service you are providing something that people will still pay money for no matter what the economy is?

Consider starting a restaurant. When times are good, people eat out all the time. They would rather pay for the convenience of somebody cooking for them because they are all too tired from working. Let's face it that is what microwave ovens are for as well. People are hungry and what instant gratification N-O-W.

What about when times are tough? The first thing that happens with most people is that they see what they can get rid of in terms of expenses. Where can they cut costs? For a lot of people that means shopping at the Dollar Tree stores and buying $1 meals. Cooking at home means they are saving money and the same goes for starting to bring a bag lunch to work instead of going out and spending anywhere from $7 to $15 for lunch like they use to.

If you are planning though on a business where you can sell inexpensive food, like a hot dog cart in a good location, you may have a recession proof business. Remember you still need to do your own due diligence and planning.

In your business plan, you need to have what your start up costs are and what your monthly overhead will be for running the business. This would be a good time to also take inventory of your monthly personal expenses because if you are planning eventually on quitting your day job (or making this new gig your new day job) you should know how much you need to live on each month.

Whatever numbers you come up with figure anywhere between 10-35% extra padding should be added to account for emergencies, holiday expenditures and if all things go well, money for expansion of your business.

Let's take the previously mentioned example of a hot dog cart. I have no idea if these numbers are realistic but they are here to serve as an illustration of start up costs:

Hot dog cart	$3000
Hot dogs	$200
Buns	$200
Condiments	$75
Business license	$25
Resale license	$0
Fliers	$100
Sodas and chips	$540
Total Start up Costs:	$4140

And we will throw in 10% emergency cash of $414 to make our total start up costs a grand total of $4554.

Let's say you need to replenish the hot dogs, buns, sodas and chips each month. I know I forgot to add napkins and aluminum foil so I can take some of that money from the emergency cash I allocated up front.

Our monthly overhead might include gasoline to drive to a location, say the front of the County Courthouse at lunch time - $300 a month.

Figure $1015 a month for expenses.

That is your monthly forecast for what you will need in the worse scenario cases if you don't even sell one hot dog. Are these acceptable costs for you and do you have the money to gut it out for 3-6 months till people see your cart and start realizing what a delicious hot dog really tastes like? What if the weather is lousy and you are stuck with rain for three months? How will you make expenses meet in the meantime since hot dogs won't keep forever and you will have to re-buy new ones?

Again, please be sure to do your research in advance and make sure that the startup costs aren't too high or that your expenses aren't going to mushroom out of control and eat up all the profits that you should be making!

Let's say that you have all the other elements for your imaginary hot dog cart business planned out. The next thing you need to take into account that should be incorporated into your business plan as well is your competition.

What are you up against in your anticipated marketplace? If you are selling hot dogs outside the city courthouse are there already three other hot dog vendors out there? Are all of them swamped at lunch and it looks like that if they had a dozen hot dog carts that they all would still be swamped?

Just because there is a lot of competition that doesn't mean that you should run away. On the contrary, that could mean that there is a huge demand for the product or service that you are trying to sell. You need to recognize though if the competition is seasonal or timely.

People won't eat dogs (usually) at 7 am in the morning if they are going to work at the courthouse. They might eat though between 11 am and 2 pm throughout the day. Maybe between 4-6 pm you might get another bump in business.

In the toy business, your seasonal sales in the United States are usually from October through December. In India, you can sell gold for weddings generally before monsoon season.

Are you also different enough from the competition to draw business to you from your competitors? Maybe you sell kosher hot dogs. Maybe you have a cute girl in a bikini serving the hot dogs. What is your edge that will differentiate you or your product from your competition?

By recognizing your competition and incorporating it in your business plan, you show potential investors that you know what you are doing or at least have researched your market enough so that they can see that you are taking yourself seriously and will be treating your job as a business!

Do you like to work long hours? Can you deal well with aggravation and stress? If you are planning on starting your own business you need to be able to deal with working ten to twelve hour work days initially. It will be your business and it will grow or wither away depending on how much time and energy you put in.

If we go back to our hot dog cart example, you can figure that you will move your cart from place to place to try and maximize the amount of hot dogs you can sell in an 8-12 hour period of time.

Let's say you need to open up your hot dog cart at the courthouse at 11 for the lunch hour rush. You are there for two hours so plan on getting an additional two hours of preparation each day to get to your first destination. From 2-4 you travel to some construction sites or to a stadium. From 4:30-6 pm you go back to the courthouse or stay at the stadium. Let us say that you move to an outdoor mall by the ocean to get the late night traffic. You end up staying there till 10 pm. You then take 1-2 hours to go home, clean up the cart and get ready for tomorrow's day.

Ask most independent businessmen and you will find that they work up 10-15 hour days easily. Most of them enjoy what they are doing so initially it isn't a problem.

But if you want to have a social life and get back to your family, girl friend, boy friend or relative of choice, you need for them to understand that initially they won't be seeing much of you because you are trying to start your own business.

Be aware that there is a relationship arc to starting a business. When you first get started you and everybody around you is excited – it is the honeymoon phase. Things then settle down into "married" mode and after that it gets to be like anything else if you aren't excited about it-the living drudgery of life.

It is better to try and do something you love so that it will minimize the living drudge factor later on.

Also you may not find friends and family getting as excited as you are about your business. If that is the case, short of getting rid of your friends and family please do something to get a support group going.

Your friends and family should be on board with you but sometimes for various reasons they will think that you are crazy. Of course, should your business take off, they will be the first to tell you that they were there from the beginning and can you either give Cousin Ernie a job or loan them a couple of thousand dollars.

In the next chapter, I will give you some ideas of what kind of jobs are out there that you might be able to get into and still be able to do.

Make Money Doing Things That People Hate To Do

You can make money in the meantime trying to do what people hate to do.

When people ask me, "Kim, what is one of the easiest ways to make money?" I have to tell them that there aren't any easy ways of making money short of inheriting it and leaving it to earn simple interest in a safe investment instrument. An easier way to make money though is finding what people hate to do and jumping into that market and doing it.

Take something simple like recycling. Back in the day, nobody wanted to haul or pick up trash. The savvy businessmen and companies that got involved in the trash hauling business discovered there was big money in contracts with other companies and even cities in disposing of garbage. The logical business after that was recycling. Getting people's garbage, sorting out what has monetary value and reselling it seems like a no-brainer during the green, ecological thinking times we are in now but the way to make money in that business is long gone. Simply put, the markets have already been mined, they are fiercely competitive and you would have to find places where it hasn't been worth somebody's business to start a trash collecting business.

The other major problem in finding businesses where people hate to have anything to do with them is that you have to make sure that there isn't a global competitor who can undercut you. Most people don't like to write computer code for example. You would think that computer programming would still pay decently and it does for some markets. If it is an up and coming computer system or product and people haven't jumped all over yet, you may have a couple of years of setting yourself up a decent practice with it. If you do good work and word gets around, you may be able to continue in the market despite saturation as more international outsourcing companies come on board to try and undercut you.

An interesting problem is that like all other products, even outsourcing gets to be expensive or not worth the aggravation if it ends up costing you clients or business. The reason some call centers are back stateside here in the U.S. is that some Americans still give good customer service over the web and phone and actually understand what your issues and concerns are.

So here is what I would do if I were young and looking for a great business move:

I would start looking at what are the junky jobs or things that people don't want to do and how much can I charge for me to do it? Is it also something I can physically (and psychologically) stomach doing even though I may be making money with it.

If you are a sewer electrician, you probably are working for utility companies or cities all the time. Not everybody is cut out for that work and it can be hazardous. Besides accidents happening underground, you can fall, get infection, possibly get electrocuted, well you get the idea.

Do you know why movie producers generally pay so little for new script writers, actors or actresses? It is because they know that there are thousands of people out there who will do that kind of work for free just to have exposure.

You will not find many people wanting to go down into a wet, cold and dark sewer to work on decaying electrical wiring and a rusted junction box for free.

Just remember in your planning to account for taxes and as usual, write your business plan down!

If you can think of any yucky jobs that people don't want to do, let me know. I know there is at least one TV show on cable about it and I suspect there will be more if nothing else just for the shock factor. For a lot of people they can live with the dirt and risk if the price is right.

The question is, is it also right for you?

Remember that start up costs are low when doing a yuck job that nobody wants to do for somebody else and you can eventually move into running your own job later on your own.

If I had to do it over again I would think about being a plumber. Even in times like this when money is tight, there are always people who don't like to get their hands dirty. In some cases, it may not be practical for them to dig up their lawn, root around for their water pipe, look for a leak, try not to hit an electrical line and replace it.

People, like you and I, who are living in a post-industrial culture like their indoor plumbing. We like to be able to go into a room like the kitchen, pull a lever and have water-clean water-dispensed to us. We like to use our toilets inside of the house as well.

When people are having serious plumbing problems, they may balk at the price but they will pay whatever it costs to stop the tree roots from invading their pipes or their laundry water from flooding their house!

If you start thinking along these lines, you will get an idea of some of the jobs that people don't want to do. Be warned that in tough economic times, people will try to learn to do things themselves to save money.

The plus side is that when they mess it up, they have to call in an expert to fix it!

Thoughts About How You Raise Money

If you have done a good job with your business plan you should have something that you can take to bankers, investors or private people to borrow money from. I will get into specific details about that in the chapter on the business plan. First, I want to get your mind thinking about raising money.

The people who will be putting up the money will want to know what their money is going to be put to use for and what kind of return they will be getting for their investment.

Here is a cosmic truth that some people know very well and others need to be reminded:

PEOPLE WILL PUT THEIR MONEY INTO SOMETHING THAT THEY THINK WILL MAKE THEM A TREMENDOUS AMOUNT OF MONEY

Think it is an obvious statement? It is beyond obvious because people are G-R-E-E-D-Y. That is why despite warnings from Better Business Bureaus, the Internet, television news teams, etc people fall for scams.

People think that they can invest one dollar and in one day get back $100. People spend billions on lottery tickets where you have the same odds of winning whether you are playing or not and they get nothing for their trouble accept losing a dollar.

How does this work in terms of your business? Bankers and relatives want to give you a dollar to make a hundred dollars and of course, know that they are not going to lose it. In other words they want a risk free investment that will return 100 times the investment.

Sounds silly? It is. Knowing this to be the case, you have to make your financial pitch being brutally honest so they can see that what you are proposing has a certain degree of risk but the rewards outweigh the risks.

People say that banks are not lending money now. Banks may have some stricter guidelines but if the loan officer sees a business where he can not only get back his loan but more than enough interest he will okay the loan.

Private parties will be happy to invest in your presentation if you can honestly show them that they will be getting a decent rate of return and their money is relatively safe.

There are the keys to your financial kingdom. You obviously can't give the proposed lender a bullet proof investment that will return buckets of money but you can show the lender a realistic investment. In this current economy a lot of people will be content will single digit returns on their investment if it is safe and there is room to grow.

If your business is something that you have a track record for making money with that is something that you need to let the potential investor know.

If you are approaching relatives, unless they are very wealthy (and even then that might be more of a hassle), you should still present everything in a realistic light (knowing that you can still put positive spins on things in your business plan and presentation).

As a business person I am all about full disclosure. That means that in your business plan (your verbal pitch), let your potential investor know how many other gigs like this succeed or fail and what the risk/reward is for them.

Without getting too deep into other forms of business entities, you may be approached to turning your business into a partnership or corporation with the investor having a certain percentage and maybe wanting to control the whole thing.

You need to weigh the best direction for you since you will be the one who ultimately will have to work under those business conditions on a daily basis. If you feel that your business has a lot more potential, then find other sources of income to get your business going.

Another interesting phenomenon which you may see happen is that once you are a success or on the track and you don't need money, people will start coming over to you and offer to help you expand, want in, they might practically be throwing cash at you.

Having people toss money at you is always a good idea but be very cautious in taking it if it will jeopardize the business model that you have that is making money.

Remember that times to get more money are when you are comfortable that your business is growing and you need the cash to keep things going and to expand your business.

Some businesses have done just fine sticking to basics and not going out of their core business despite market competition. In and Out Burger comes to mind that they haven't budged from their basic format of burgers, fries, sodas and shakes. Their menu is basic but there are always lines of cars going through their drive thru windows and their recipe for success hasn't changed.

Don't be fooled by the lure of money if that will clobber your business in the long run. If somebody wants to buy you out, congratulations, just run the numbers and make sure that is something that you want to do and get started on getting your next business ready. People might be waiting to invest with you again since you have a track record of having hits.

After all nothing feeds success like success, right?

What's An Exit Strategy?

When planning a business it is a good idea to also think about what your exit strategy is. An exit strategy is a plan for gracefully (and sometimes awkwardly) leaving your business. It can be either by selling it, giving it to your kids (who will probably run it into the ground unless you teach them how to run it) or even keep the business your whole life.

Your reasons for starting your business may be because you genuinely love what you do or maybe you have a certain dollar amount that you are looking for to retire on. Once you hit that in savings, maybe you don't want to have to work for a living anymore. If you can hit your goal like that, more power to you!

Other important factors are what will happen if things start to go south and the business isn't making money. At what point if you aren't turning a profit are you going to decide to shut things down? What if you start to have losses of $1000 a month? Can you handle losses of $10,000 a month?

Plan for how you will shut things down, liquidate assets and know where your exit door is on you business now. Being in debt is not fun.

It is a lot easier to prepare in advance so you don't have to agonize over it later on in case your business is losing money and there isn't a valid financial reason to keep it going.

What's A Sole Proprietorship and Why Do I Want One?

Good question. Maybe like lots of us you've just been laid off. Maybe you are out of luck because a lot of companies are making do with what they have and they may not be interested in hiring you because you are considered too young, too old, too expensive, too aggressive, too passive, too too-muchiness. Who knows?

Maybe you are working at a fast food restaurant window and are realizing that you need to get something going to realize your lifelong dream as a barber.

Americans have a long tradition of starting up their own businesses. When you run your own business and you are your own boss, the easiest (relatively speaking) business entity you can have is a sole proprietorship.

Think of it. You set your own hours, you set your own prices and you are the master of your own fate.

Unfortunately the reality is that people who run their own businesses work harder than people who are wage slaves (they receive W-2 income) and often aren't making enough as if they were working for somebody else.

So, why would anybody want to do it? As mentioned in the beginning of the chapter, you may not have a choice. If financially you have this as your only means of making a living, you may as well make the best of it and go forward armed with the information you need to become a success.

It is also an opportunity because you can move forward doing what you may have wanted to do most of your life. It may seem scary at first but like anything else, it is just unfamiliarity that is spooky.

One of my great success story secrets is that I spend a lot of time deciding what businesses to not go into. Just because somebody else can make money doing it doesn't mean that I can. I may not have the marketing chops, maybe the market situation has changed (for example, the type of haircuts I offer aren't popular anymore and I don't know how to cut hair any other way) or maybe I can't stand what it is that I wanted to do once I started doing it. It happens.

I use to love collecting comic books but once I started selling comics and collectibles I started looking at comic books as just things to sell. It was the easiest way to kill a hobby that I loved.

This book may also help you realize that perhaps being your own boss isn't the right career path for you. That is okay as well. It is better to be out the cost of the book then sink thousands of dollars and hundreds of hours of time into a business that you find out you hate doing.

Sometimes some great ideas come out of hobbies or off shoots of their jobs. Ray Kroc approached the McDonald brothers to go into business with them because back in the day they were selling hamburgers, fries and shakes. Ray is my hero because he didn't get started in making his millions until he was considered old.

Be willing to cast aside previously held notions though once you decide you are going to transition from having a hobby into turning into a business.

In running a business there are very distinct guidelines and goals that you need to meet not the least is actually making money and not running the business as if it were a hobby.

Are you a Hobby or a Business?

In my book, "Bad Tax Idea, Good Tax Idea", I touched on the importance of running your business, er, like a business. If you don't follow my advice or the appropriate guidelines in determining whether an activity is a business or a hobby, an activity not engaged in for profit, the IRS may make the determination for you - and in a way that you won't like.

In order to educate ourselves regarding our obligations, let us take a look at the big picture and see what the IRS is dealing with and why they tend to get so cranky about incorrect designations of hobbies or businesses. Incorrect deduction of hobby expenses account for a portion of the overstated adjustments, deductions, exemptions and credits that add up to $30 billion per year in unpaid taxes, according to IRS estimates.

In general, taxpayers may deduct ordinary and necessary expenses for conducting a trade or business. An ordinary expense is an expense that is common and accepted in the taxpayer's trade or business. A necessary expense is one that is appropriate for the business. Generally, an activity qualifies as a business if it is carried on with the reasonable expectation of earning a profit.

In order to make this determination, we should consider the following factors:

1. Does the time and effort put into the activity indicate an intention to make a profit?
2. Does the taxpayer depend on income from the activity?
3. If there are losses, are they due to circumstances beyond the taxpayer's control or did they occur in the start-up phase of the business?
4. Has the taxpayer changed methods of operation to improve profitability?
5. Does the taxpayer or his/her advisors have the knowledge needed to carry on the activity as a successful business?

6. Has the taxpayer made a profit in similar activities in the past?
7. Does the activity make a profit in some years?
8. Can the taxpayer expect to make a profit in the future from the appreciation of assets used in the activity?
9. Are you doing this because it gives you personal pleasure or recreation?

The IRS presumes that an activity is carried on for profit if it makes a profit during at least three of the last five tax years, including the current year — at least two of the last seven years for activities that consist primarily of breeding, showing, training or racing horses.

A further break down of the nine questions that the IRS uses to help determine if you are a business or hobby goes as follows:

1. Businesslike Manner. Importance is placed on whether the tax-payer carries on the activity in a businesslike manner. If the taxpayer carries on the activity in a businesslike manner, he or she is more likely to convince the IRS, or the tax court, that the activity is for profit.
Keeping good records, maintaining separate personal and business checking accounts, and having a written business plan are all indicative of a profit motive. So are marketing efforts that establish you are trying to get out there and sell your product or service!

Changing the methods of operating the activity to reduce costs or increase revenues can be evidence of a profit motive.

Under certain circumstances, ceasing operations altogether can be evidence of a profit motive. That has happened in Tax Court where the Court ruled that proof of the fact that the person was running a business was closing it down because he realized that to continue would lose money.

In the case of a person named Sampson, Tax Court Memo 1982-276, the taxpayer who bred, raised, and trained wolf dogs was found to have a profit motive. One factor in his favor was that he ceased operations when his expenses got out of hand – his dogs were chewing through a chain-link fence and attacking his neighbor's cattle.

He showed that he was a smart businessman who wasn't continuing to lose money (especially with the risk of lawsuits for the wolf dogs eating more than cattle).

TAX LAW, AS STRANGE AS IT MAY SEEM, REWARDS COMMON SENSE AND PUNISHES STUPIDITY

It may seem obvious after the fact but think about things logically and you will get an idea that not all the tax laws are completely crazy.

2. Expertise. Importance is placed on whether the taxpayers, or the taxpayer's advisors, have the expertise needed to carry on the activity as a successful business. The more expertise a taxpayer has, the more likely the IRS will find a profit motive. Seeking knowledge through study or consultation with experts also indicates a profit motive.

If you as a business person study and consult with experts - you better take their advice otherwise will have difficulty showing a profit motive if he or she fails to follow the practices recommended. Make sure that your experts know what they are talking about!!

3. Time and Effort. Importance is placed on the amount of time and effort the taxpayer devotes to carrying on the activity. This is especially true if the activity does not have substantial recreational aspects. A taxpayer who leaves an occupation to pursue the activity may be more likely to be viewed as having

a profit motive. Also a taxpayer may show profit motive by employing others who invest time and effort in the activity.

4. Expectation of Appreciation. Importance is placed on whether the taxpayer can expect to make a future profit from the appreciation of the assets of the activity. The taxpayer's expected profit from the activity can include the potential increase in the value of assets used in the activity.

5. Success in Other Activities. Importance is placed on whether the taxpayer was successful in making a profit in other activities in the past. If the taxpayer was profitable in a similar activity, it may indicate he or she is engaged in the present activity for profit.

Prior experience, however, can be a double-edged sword. When a tax-payer has previous experience in a similar activity which was a hobby, the court is likely to rule that the current activity is a hobby as well.

6. History of Income and Losses. Importance is placed on the history of the income and losses of the activity. A series of years where there was profit would indicate a profit motive. On the other hand, ongoing losses undermine the claim of a profit motive. Although, they do not necessarily disprove a profit motive.
Losses beyond the control of the taxpayer do not indicate a lack of profit motive. Examples of losses beyond the control of the taxpayer include drought, disease, fire, theft, weather damage, involuntary conversion, and depressed market conditions.

Also, appropriate losses in the start-up phase of a business do not necessarily indicate a lack of profit motive. The amount of time necessary to reach profitability varies with the type of activity. Farming, inventing, and artistic endeavors are some examples of activities where diligent effort over a long period of time is often necessary before profits are made.

7. Occasional Profits. Importance is placed on whether the activity makes a profit in some years and the amount of the profits. The amount of profits in relation to the amount of losses incurred may provide useful information in determining the taxpayer's intent. Also, the amount of the taxpayer's investment and the value of the assets compared to the profits can be used to assess the profit motive.

An occasional small profit from an activity in which the taxpayer has made a large investment generally would not demonstrate a profit motive. However, an occasional substantial profit (compared to investment) generally would indicate an activity is engaged in for profit. Even an opportunity to earn a substantial latter profit in a speculative venture is usually sufficient to indicate the activity is engaged in for profit.

8. Dependency on Income. Importance is placed on whether the taxpayer depends on the income from the activity for his or her livelihood. The fact that the taxpayer does not have substantial income or capital from sources other than the activity may indicate the activity is engaged in for profit. On the other hand, income coming in from other sources may indicate the activity is not engaged in for profit. The IRS has been particularly skeptical when the losses from the activity generate large tax benefits.
Again, that is something to keep in mind - keep things in the realm of reality, not the realm of impossibility. Figure that the IRS has heard it ALL before!

9. Element of Personal Pleasure. Importance is placed on whether the taxpayer is in the activity for personal pleasure or recreation. The mere fact that the taxpayer enjoys his or her activity does not mean it will be treated as a hobby. Nevertheless, elements of personal pleasure can have a detrimental impact on establishing a profit motive, and the absence of pleasure can help establish a profit motive.

If an activity is not for profit, losses from that activity may not be used to offset other income. An activity produces a loss when related expenses exceed income. The limit on not-for-profit losses applies to individuals, partnerships, estates, trusts, and S corporations. It does not apply to corporations other than S corporations.

Deductions for hobby activities are claimed as itemized deductions on Schedule A (Form 1040). These deductions must be taken in the following order and only to the extent stated in each of three categories:

1. Deductions that a taxpayer may take for personal as well as business activities, such as home mortgage interest and taxes, may be taken in full.
2. Deductions that don't result in an adjustment to basis, such as advertising, insurance premiums and wages, may be taken next, to the extent gross income for the activity is more than the deductions from the first category.
3. Business deductions that reduce the basis of property, such as depreciation and amortization, are taken last, but only to the extent gross income for the activity is more than the deductions taken in the first two categories.

My best practices suggestion for anybody going into a business is to constantly try to keep demonstrating that you are serious about the business and running it so that you can make a profit.

The rule of thumb also for wanting to take a position is now fifty-fifty. That means that if you think that you have a fifty-fifty chance of taking the position that you are and that it would stick if the IRS challenges it, you may be denied but you won't be considered having trying to do something illegal, if that makes sense.

The key thing to remember would be to make it reasonable.

What is reasonable for one business may not be reasonable for another. One example can be that a roofer may have a lot of small tools as expenses since he leaves behind and loses lots of screwdrivers, hammers and the like on projects. If you are a gourmet chef you cannot deduct the same items unless you are making some incredibly inedible dishes.

The IRS understands that some businesses may take awhile to turn a profit but the bottom line is that if you aren't making money at the business that you should get out of the business. The reasonable and sane person doesn't keep throwing away money into a gig that is losing money.

If you are a video game tester for a living you might be able to deduct expenses paid for buying games. If you are an attorney, unless the video game was key evidence in a case, you would be hard pressed to try to justify it in an audit.

Not only will the IRS disallow the items you may find that you have called unwanted attention to yourself and they might start digging for things that had nothing to do with your business.

Of course you have nothing to hide, but why go through all the aggravation and time wasted in trying to defend a position that you shouldn't have been challenged on in the first place?

I may have mentioned before but it bears repeating that if you live in a state where there are state income taxes you can also be subject to having your state taxes amended since the Federal government is doing a better job with communicating with the state taxing authorities.

What's A Business Plan?

What's a business plan? It is a blueprint you need to run your business. It is making formal your road map to success. Before you start a business you need to have your path planned out.

In order to present yourself to the public, to potential investors or partners (think money people – like a bank) or potential people who will extend you credit (money people again) you need to show them that you mean business.

You should have the goal or purpose of what you are trying to do spelled out clearly. Your business plan should have the elements that show that you know what you are talking about and that you are serious about going into business.

It should also change and grow to reflect your growth with your business.

Your business plan should contain the following:

Business Plan Executive Summary
The executive summary is part 1 of the business plan and is the most important section of your plan. It provides a concise overview of the entire plan, along with a history of your business. This section tells your reader where your gig is and where you want to take it. It's the first thing your readers see; therefore, it is the thing that will either grab their interest and make them want to keep reading or make them want to put it down and forget about it. More than anything else, this section is important because it tells the reader why you think your business idea will be successful.

The executive summary should be the last section you write. After you've worked out all the details of your plan, you'll be in a better position to summarize it--and it should be a summary (for example, no more than four pages in length).

Contents of the Executive Summary

The Mission Statement -- The mission statement briefly explains the thrust of your business. It could be two words, two sentences, a paragraph, or even a single image. It should be as direct and focused as possible, and it should leave the reader with a clear picture of what your business is all about.

a. Date the business began
b. Names of the founders and the functions they perform
c. Number of employees
d. Location of the business and any branches or subsidiaries
e. Description of plant or facilities
f. Products manufactured/services rendered
g. Banking relationships and information regarding current investors
h. Summary of business growth including financial or market highlights (for example, your business doubled its worth in a 12-month period; you became the first business in your industry to provide a certain service)
i. Summary of management's future plans. With the exception of the Mission Statement, all of the information in the Executive Summary should be highlighted in a brief, even bulleted, fashion. Remember, these facts are laid out in-depth within the plan itself.

If you're just starting a business, you won't have a lot of information to plug into the areas mentioned above. Instead, focus on your experience and background as well as the decisions that led you to start this particular enterprise. Include information about the problems your target market has and what solutions you provide. Show how the expertise you have will allow you to make significant inroads into the market. Tell your reader what you're going to do differently or better. Convince the reader that there is a need for your service or product, then go ahead and address your future plans.

Market Analysis

The market analysis section is Part 2 of the business plan. This section should illustrate your knowledge about the particular industry your business is in. It should also present general highlights and conclusions of any marketing research data you have collected; however, the specific details of your marketing research studies should be moved to the appendix section of your business plan.
This section should include: an industry description and outlook, target market information, market test results, lead times, and an evaluation of your competition.

Industry Description and Outlook
This overview section should include: a description of your primary industry, the current size of the industry as well as its historic growth rate, trends and characteristics related to the industry as a whole (i.e., What life cycle stage is the industry in? What is its projected growth rate?), and the major customer groups within the industry (i.e., businesses, governments, consumers, etc).

Identifying Your Target Market
Your target market is simply the market (or group of customers) that you want to target (or focus on and sell to). When you are defining your target market, it is important to narrow it to a manageable size. Many businesses make the mistake of trying to be everything to everybody. Often times, this philosophy leads to failure.

In this section, you should gather information which identifies the following:

1. Distinguishing characteristics of the major/primary market you are targeting. This section might include information about the critical needs of your potential customers, the degree to which those needs are (or are not) currently being met, and the demographics of the group. It would also include the geographic location of

your target market, the identification of the major decision-makers, and any seasonal or cyclical trends which may impact the industry or your business.

2. Size of the primary target market. Here, you would need to know the number of potential customers in your primary market, the number of annual purchases they make in products or services similar to your own, the geographic area they reside in, and the forecasted market growth for this group.

3. The extent to which you feel you will be able to gain market share and the reasons why. In this research, you would determine the market share percentage and number of customers you expect to obtain in a defined geographic area. You would also outline the logic you used to develop these estimates.

4. Your pricing and gross margin targets. Here, you would define the levels of your pricing, your gross margin levels, and any discount structures that you plan to set up for your business, such as volume/bulk discounts or prompt payment discounts.

5. Resources for finding information related to your target market. These resources might include directories, trade association publications, and government documents.

6. Media you will use to reach your target audience. These might include publications, radio or television broadcasts, or any other type of credible source that may have influence with your target market.

7. Purchasing cycle of your potential customers. You will need to identify the needs of your target market, do research to find the solutions to their needs, evaluate the solutions you come up with, and finally, identify who actually has the authority to choose the final solution.

Trends and potential changes which may impact your primary target market, along with key characteristics of your secondary markets. Just like with your primary target market, you would again want to identify the needs, demographics and the significant trends which will influence your secondary markets in the future.

Market Tests

When you are including information about any of the market tests you have completed for your business plan, be sure to focus only on the results of these tests. Any specific details should be included in the appendix. Market test results might include: the potential customers who were contacted, any information or demonstrations that were given to prospective customers, how important it is to satisfy the target market's needs, and the target market's desire to purchase your business' products or services at varying prices.

Lead Times

Lead time is the amount of time between when a customer places an order and when the product or service is actually delivered. When you are researching this information, determine what your lead time will be for the initial order, reorders and volume purchases.

Competitive Analysis

When you are doing a competitive analysis, you need to identify your competition by product line or service as well as by market segment; assess their strengths and weaknesses, determine how important your target market is to your competitors, and identify any barriers which may hinder you as you are entering the market.

Be sure to identify all of your key competitors for each of your products or services. For each key competitor, determine what their market share is, then try to estimate how long it will take before new competitors will enter into the marketplace. In other words, what is your window of opportunity? Finally, identify any indirect or secondary competitors which may have an impact on your business' success.

The strengths of your competitors are also competitive advantages which you, too, can provide. The strengths of your competitors may take many forms, but the most common include:

1. An ability to satisfy customer needs

2. A large share of the market and the consumer awareness that comes with it

3. A good track record and reputation

4. Solid financial resources and the subsequent staying power which that provides

Competitor's Weaknesses

Weaknesses are simply the flip side of strengths. In other words, analyze the same areas as you did before to determine what your competitors' weaknesses are. Are they unable to satisfy their customers' needs? Do they have poor market penetration? Is their track record or reputation not up to par? Do they have limited financial resources? Can they not retain good people? All of these can be red flags for any business. If you find weak areas in your competition, be sure to find out why they are having problems. This way, you can avoid the same mistakes they have made.

If your target market is not important to your competition, then you will most likely have an open field to run in if your idea is a good one -- at least for a while. However, if the competition is keen for your target market, be prepared to overcome some barriers.

Barriers to any market might include:

1. A high investment cost

2. The time it takes to set up your business

3. Changing technology

4. The lack of quality personnel

5. Customer resistance (i.e., long-standing relationships, brand loyalty)

6. Existing patents and trademarks that you can not infringe upon

Regulatory Restrictions

The final area that you should look at as you're researching this section is regulatory restrictions. This includes information related to current customer or governmental regulatory requirements as well as any changes that may be upcoming. Specific details that you need to find out include: the methods for meeting any of the requirements which will affect your business, the timing involved (i.e., How long do you have to comply? When do the requirements go into effect?), and the costs involved.

Business Description

The business description is Part 3 of the business plan. Without going into detail, this section should include a high level look at how all of the different elements of your business fit together. The business description section should include information about the nature of your business as well as list the primary factors that you believe will make your business a success.

When defining the nature of your business (or why you're in business), be sure to list the marketplace needs that you are trying to satisfy. This should include the ways in which you plan to satisfy these needs using your products or services. Finally, list the specific individuals and/or organizations that you have identified as having these needs.

Organization & Management

Organization and Management is Part 4 of the business plan. This section should include: your business's organizational structure, details about the ownership of your business, profiles of your management team, and your qualifications. Who does what in your business? What is their background and why are you bringing them into the business as contractors, members or employees? What are they responsible for? These may seem like unnecessary questions to answer in a one- or two-person organization, but the people reading your business plan want to know who's in charge, so tell them. Give a detailed description of each division or department and its function.

This section should include who's on the board (if you have an advisory board) and how you intend to keep them there. What kind of salary and benefits package do you have for your people? What incentives are you offering? How about promotions? Reassure your reader that the people you have on staff are more than just names on a letterhead.

Organizational Structure

A simple but effective way to lay out the structure of your firm is to create an organizational chart with a narrative description. This will prove that you're leaving nothing to chance, you've thought out exactly who is doing what, and there is someone in charge of every function of your business. Nothing will fall through the cracks, and nothing will be done three or four times over. To a potential investor or employee, that is very important.

Ownership Information

This section should also include the legal structure of your business along with the subsequent ownership information it relates to. Have you incorporated your business? If so, is it a C or S corporation? Or perhaps you have formed a partnership with someone. If so, is it a general or limited partnership? Or maybe you are a sole proprietor.

Important ownership information that should be incorporated into your business plan includes:

1. Names of owners-should be you and your wife if you are doing a sole proprietorship. If you opt to change to another business entity later on you can change it accordingly.

2. Percentage ownership

3. Extent of involvement with the business

4. Forms of ownership (i.e., common stock, preferred stock, general partner, limited partner)

5. Outstanding equity equivalents (i.e., options, warrants, convertible debt)

6. Common stock (i.e., authorized or issued)

Management Profiles

Experts agree that one of the strongest factors for success in any growth business is the ability and track record of its owner/management team, so let your reader know about the key people in your business and their backgrounds.

Provide resumes that include the following information:

1. Name

2. Position (include brief position description along with primary duties)

3. Primary responsibilities and authority

4. Education

5. Unique experience and skills

6. Prior employment

7. Special skills

8. Past track record

9. Industry recognition

10. Community involvement

11. Number of years with business

12. Compensation basis and levels (make sure these are reasonable -- not too high or too low)

Be sure you quantify achievements (e.g. "Managed a sales force of ten people," "Managed a department of fifteen people," "Increased revenue by 15 percent in the first six months," "Expanded the retail outlets at the rate of two each year," "Improved the customer service as rated by our customers from a 60 percent to a 90 percent rating").

Also highlight how the people surrounding you complement your own skills. If you're just starting out, show how each person's unique experience will contribute to the success of your venture.

Board of Directors' Qualifications

For a sole prop you really don't have a Board of Directors but you can mention advisors. The major benefit of an unpaid advisory board is that it can provide expertise that your business cannot otherwise afford. A list of well-known, successful business owners/managers can go a long way toward enhancing your gig's credibility and perception of management expertise.

If you later on have a board of directors, be sure to gather the following information when developing the outline for your business plan:

1. Names
2. Positions on the board
3. Extent of involvement with business
4. Background
5. Historical and future contribution to the business's success

Marketing & Sales Management

Marketing and Sales Strategies is Part 5 of your business plan. Marketing is the process of creating customers, and customers are the lifeblood of your business. In this section, the first thing you want to do is define your marketing strategy. There is no single way to approach a marketing strategy; your strategy should be part of an ongoing business-evaluation process and unique to your business. However, there are common steps you can follow which will help you think through the direction and tactics you would like to use to drive sales and sustain customer loyalty.

An overall marketing strategy should include four different strategies:

1. A market penetration strategy.

2. A growth strategy. This strategy for building your business might include: an internal strategy such as how to increase your human resources, an acquisition strategy such as buying another business, a franchise strategy for branching out, a horizontal strategy where you would provide the same type of products to different users, or a vertical strategy where you would continue providing the same products but would offer them at different levels of the distribution chain.

3. Channels of distribution strategy. Choices for distribution channels could include original equipment manufacturers (OEMs), an internal sales force, distributors, or retailers.

4. Communication strategy. How are you going to reach your customers? Usually a combination of the following tactics works the best: promotions, advertising, public relations, personal selling, and printed materials such as brochures, catalogs, flyers, etc.

After you have developed a comprehensive marketing strategy, you can then define your sales strategy. This covers how you plan to actually sell your product.

Your overall sales strategy should include two primary elements:

A sales force strategy. If you are going to have a sales force, do you plan to use internal or independent representatives? How many salespeople will you recruit for your sales force? What type of recruitment strategies will you use? How will you train your sales force? What about compensation for your sales force?

Your sales activities. When you are defining your sales strategy, it is important that you break it down into activities. For instance, you need to identify your prospects. Once you have made a list of your prospects, you need to prioritize the contacts, selecting the leads with the highest potential to buy first. Next, identify the number of sales calls you will make over a certain period of time. From there, you need to determine the average number of sales calls you will need to make per sale, the average dollar size per sale, and the average dollar size per vendor.

Service or Product Line

Service or Product Line is Part 6 of your business plan. What are you selling? In this section, describe your service or product, emphasizing the benefits to potential and current customers. For example, don't tell your readers which 89 foods you carry in your "Gourmet to Go" shop. Tell them why busy, two-career couples will prefer shopping in a service-oriented store that records peoples' food preferences and caters even the smallest parties on short notice.

Focus on the areas where you have a distinct advantage. Identify the problem in your target market for which your service or product provides a solution. Give the reader hard evidence that people are, or will be, willing to pay for your solution. List your business's services and products and attach any marketing/promotional materials. Provide details regarding suppliers, availability of products/services, and service or product costs. Also include information addressing new services or products which will soon be added to the business's line.

Overall, this section should include:

1. A detailed description of your product or service (from your customers' perspective). You should include information about the specific benefits of your product or service. You should also talk about your

product/service's ability to meet consumer needs, any advantages your product has over that of the competition, and the present development stage your product is in (i.e. idea, prototype, etc.).

2. Information related to your product's life cycle. Be sure to include information about where your product or service is in its life cycle, as well as any factors that may influence its cycle in the future.

3. Any copyright, patent, and trade secret information that may be relevant. This should include information related to existing, pending, or anticipated copyright and patent filings along with any key characteristics of your products/services that you cannot obtain a copyright or patent for. This is where you should also incorporate key aspects of your products/services that may be classified as trade secrets. Last, but not least, be sure to add any information pertaining to existing legal agreements, such as nondisclosure or noncompeting agreements.

4. Research and development (R&D) activities you are involved in or are planning to be involved in. These would include any in-process or future activities related to the development of new products/services. This section would also include information about what you expect the results of future R&D activities to be. Be sure to analyze the R&D efforts of not only your own business, but also that of others in your industry.

Funding Request

The Funding Request is Part 7 of your business plan. In this section, you will request the amount of funding you will need to start or expand your business. If necessary, you can include different funding scenarios, such as a best and worst case scenarios, but remember that later, in the financial section, you must be able to back up these requests and scenarios with corresponding financial statements.

You will want to include the following in your funding request: your current funding requirement, your future funding requirements over the next five years, how you will use the funds you receive, and any long-range financial strategies that you are planning that would have any type of impact on your funding request. When you are outlining your current and future funding requirements, be sure to include the amount you want now and the amount you want in the future, the time period that each request will cover, the type of funding you would like to have (i.e., equity, debt), and the terms that you would like to have applied.

How you will use your funds is very important to a creditor. Is the funding request for capital expenditures? Working capital? Debt retirement? Acquisitions? Whatever it is, be sure to list it in this section.

Last of all, make sure that you include any strategic information related to your business that may have an impact on your financial situation in the future, such as: going public with your business, having a leveraged buyout, being acquired by another business, the method with which you will service your debt, or whether or not you plan to sell your business in the future. Each of these are extremely important to a future creditor, since they will directly impact your ability to repay your loan(s).

Financials

Financials is Part 8 of your business plan. The financials should be developed after you've analyzed the market and set clear objectives. That's when you can allocate resources efficiently. The following is a list of the critical financial statements to include in your business plan packet.

Historical Financial Data

If you own an established business, you will be requested to supply historical data related to your business's performance.

Most creditors request data for the last three to five years, depending on the length of time you have been in business. The historical financial data you would want to include would be your business's income statements, balance sheets, and cash flow statements for each year you have been in business (usually for up to three to five years). Often creditors are also interested in any collateral that you may have that could be used to ensure your loan, regardless of the stage of your business.

Prospective Financial Data

All businesses, whether startup or growing, will be required to supply prospective financial data. Most of the time, creditors will want to see what you expect your business to be able to do within the next five years. Each year's documents should include forecasted income statements, balance sheets, cash flow statements, and capital expenditure budgets. For the first year, you should supply monthly or quarterly projections. After that, you can stretch it to quarterly and/or yearly projections for years two through five.
Make sure that your projections match your funding requests; creditors will be on the lookout for inconsistencies. It's much better if you catch mistakes before they do. If you have made assumptions in your projections, be sure to summarize what you have assumed. This way, the reader will not be left guessing.
Finally, include a short analysis of your financial information. Include a ratio and trend analysis for all of your financial statements (both historical and prospective). Since pictures speak louder than words, you may want to add graphs of your trend analysis (especially if they are positive).

Appendix

The Appendix is Part 9 of your business plan. This section should be provided to readers on an as-needed basis. In other words, it should not be included with the main body of your business plan. Your plan is your communication tool; as such,

it will be seen by a lot of people. Some of the information in the business section you will not want everyone to see, but, specific individuals (such as creditors) may want access to this information in order to make lending decisions. Therefore, it is important to have the appendix within easy reach.
The appendix would include:

1. Credit history (personal & business)

2. Resumes of key managers

3. Product pictures

4. Letters of reference

5. Details of market studies

6. Relevant magazine articles or book references

7. Licenses, permits or patents

8. Legal documents

9. Copies of leases

10. Building permits

11. Contracts

12. List of business consultants, including attorney and accountant

Any copies of your business plan should be controlled; keep a distribution record. This will allow you to update and maintain your business plan on an as-needed basis. Remember, too, that you should include a private placement disclaimer with your business plan if you plan to use it to raise capital.

Reporting Requirements For Federal Taxes

Let us say that your business has been going on for at least a year. That means that sooner or later it is income tax time. What do we need to file for our sole proprietorship business?

You will need to file a Fed Form 1040 and for your business, a Schedule C.

Schedule C reports income or loss from a business a person operated or a profession they practiced as a sole proprietor. One of the important questions is what is considered a business?

An activity qualifies as a business if the primary purpose for engaging in the activity is for income or profit and the person is involved in the activity with continuity and regularity. For example, if you do something once in awhile or a hobby does not qualify as a business.

One of the important aspects of filing a tax return that people mess up on is that a separate Schedule C is prepared for each distinct business activity in which a sole proprietor is engaged.

That means no combining together of income from different activities. For example, income from my software design business should not be mixed with my barber shop income. No co-mingling, please.

To be considered distinct, the activity must be a completely different business and must maintain a separate set of books. If each spouse in a married couple filing Married Filing Jointly (MFJ) has their own business, each files a separate Schedule C.

Want a great way to save money and aggravation (well, hopefully) if you are married?

You can qualify to file as a qualified joint venture.

An unincorporated business jointly owned by a married couple is generally classified as a partnership. The couple, in this case, would file Form 1065, U.S. Return of Partnership Income. That is a level of complexity that also requires other requirements at tax time and I want you to try for simplicity at first.
If I haven't mentioned this before, one of the worse mistakes people can make is forming a financial entity that they don't need and ends up costing them money.

So, where was I? Ah, qualified joint venturing... For tax years beginning after December 31, 2006, a “qualified joint venture,” whose only members are a husband and a wife filing a joint return, may elect not to be treated as a partnership.
A qualified joint venture is a joint venture that conducts a trade or business for which all of the following are true:
* The only members of the joint venture are a husband and wife who file a joint return.
* Both spouses materially participate in the trade or business.
* Both spouses elect not to be treated as a partnership.
A qualified joint venture includes only businesses that are owned and operated by spouses as co-owners, and not in the name of a state law entity (including a general or limited partnership or limited liability company). For California for example, you can elect at the Federal level to be treated as a disregarded entity if you are an LLC but you still are on the hook as of 2010 for $800 for corporate taxes. This is something again to research and watch out for if you don't want to start up with a lot of extra costs that you don't need.

Be advised that if you are trying not to be treated as a partnership, just having joint ownership of property that is not a trade or business does not qualify for the election.

The spouses must share the items of income, gain, loss, deduction, and credit in accordance with each spouse’s interest in the business.

If you aren't sure if any of this, you may want to consult a tax advisor you can trust.

Spouses make the election on a jointly filed Form 1040 by dividing all items of income, gain, loss, deduction, and credit between them in accordance with each spouse's respective interest in the joint venture.

Each spouse files a separate Schedule C, and, if required, a separate Schedule SE for Self Employment. Once made, the election can be revoked only with permission from the IRS. However, the election technically remains in effect only as long as the couple meets the requirements. If they fail to meet the requirements in one year, they will need to make the election again if they qualify in the future.

Why do couples do this? Generally it has been my experience that they do it for the wrong reasons. They generally get bad investment or business advice or try to protect assets in places like community property states where they are still stuck with having to split their issues fifty - fifty. As I stated before, when in doubt, check with a tax professional or an attorney.

Know Your Market

One of the most important things you can do to ensure that your business is going to be a hit is to know your market. You should know the people you are trying to sell your goods or services to.

That sounds like simple advice, doesn't it?

Yet every year millions of people ignore it and just go on either their gut instincts or on what they think the market should be.

The best way to know your market is to review research, talk to people in the business that you are thinking of getting in or have worked in the business before. Talk with your customers.

Let's take a classic and very current way of making money (or not making money as it were).

The online store.

Everybody and is brother, sister, dog and cat has heard or set up an online store at some point. Some people swear by them that they make a lot of money just acting as independent third parties for brokering business deals, having goods manufactured overseas shipped to the United States, making money on mark up, you name it, they have made money on it. A lot of software companies have a vested interest (as well as banks) because they want to tie you in with their services through your website or web store. Basically, it is a giant leech festival.

Another business that has had a huge share of failures over the last few years is the dollar store.

People start up a store, buy large odd lots and sell things starting at a dollar.

What do both businesses have in common?

In both cases, the store owners lose money and go out of business pretty quickly most of the time. The reasons can be many but several easy ones surface pretty quickly:

1. The owners didn't research their markets themselves and found that they were either priced out of the market or they came in as the market was dying.
2. Something changed in the environment (maybe the other stores on the block of the dollar store closed) and customers no longer want to shop there.
3. The owners aren't continuously looking to improve their inventory and respond to their customers' needs.
4. The owners have spent more on their businesses than they needed to.

For both online and brick & mortar stores you need to know your customers and have a wide variety of items to sell. For websites, unless you have a strong following, constant great prices and products, your customer base will eventually dry up and go to the next big thing.

The old way of making money through sales – have a great product, with a decent mark-up and killer customer service- still holds true today. People are price conscious but if the product they get for their money is lousy, they won't order anything like it again.

Take for example shoes. Have you ever bought a pair of low cost shoes and found that they wore out within a year instead of several years because the quality of the shoe was poor? It happens all the time.
People will spend more (especially ladies) for a higher quality shoe if it will fit, look good and last.

So whatever business it is that you are planning on starting, take some time and see what is a hit and a miss and what are the trends that are happening that could impact your business. Right now, as of the writing of this book, there is a lot of turmoil in the marketplace.

People are tight with their money but they always find some money for some of the things they like to do or can justify. Take for example designer or pretentious coffee. People have no problem spending $3.50 for a cup of coffee they could make at home for about a dollar. To them it is a treat and people will always find money to put aside to reward themselves with.

This is true in a bad economy and a depression because people will need to feel better. They try to self medicate by spending their money. That is why so many people are in debt.

Eventually people hit a wall and they realize they don't have any more money or credit to spend so that is when they cut out their special hobby or addiction as best as they can.

While doing your marketing one of the questions you need to ask yourself is what can I do to make my experience so wonderful or unique that customers will keep coming back to me even if I cost a little more?

Are you offering killer service or a one-in-a-kind warranty to back up your product or service?

Do you and your staff take the time to welcome clients, thank them and do all the things that the Internet doesn't to make them feel like they are people instead of just somebody coming to buy stuff from? People like to be treated as people.

Why do people come to me to have their income taxes done when they can do it for free or possibly cheaper using software?

I can handle tax returns that are complex that they themselves might have problems with, I treat each person with respect and trust, I take the time to give appropriate advice to each one of them that fits their specific situation and I ask for referrals.

The best marketing you can get from anybody is:

WORD OF MOUTH ADVERTISING

If you take a look at the websites and social media sites that haven't been gamed too much (meaning that friends and sponsors have fake referrals etc) you will find that word of mouth has a lot of punch in both the virtual community and our real world community.

People ask me for advice on who to ask for doing plumbing, where to shop for certain things, which websites do I go to – so the not-so-secret secret is to do a spectacular job so that you will get the referral business.

It may not happen overnight but it will happen if you are offering a quality product that is priced for your market.

No matter how great a job you are doing if your prices are so far out of line of what people can afford to pay, they will stop seeing you eventually if they start to run out of money.

Based on my limited experience I will even state that people who make a lot of money at some points get very tight with their cash and even though they expect to be paid a lot of money for their services they tend to value others services as not worth paying a lot for. It is a weird dynamic and that isn't always the case but it seems to be true especially for people who leave beyond their means on their salaries.

If you are doing your own research in a market, you should be able to adjust your product and pricing for your customers and take into account at what levels do you either increase prices or decide to get out of the business completely.

Let us say that you want to open a sandwich shop. You are near a school and you are pricing the sandwiches at a fair price, you have a fair mark up and you give discounts to the local school teams, school events and offer catering rates.

You should be able to make a living if you are working with your local community and responding to what their needs are.

You should be managing factors that you may not be able to control – rent for your store, price of produce like lettuce, price of meat, vendor supply chains, etc.

All of this is interconnected in marketing and it is something that you need to take into account when you are deciding to start a business or determining where to go with an existing gig.

****

BUSINESS FASHION TIP:

You can always test the waters by trying the business part time if you have a full time job that is making enough income to support yourself with. If there isn't a choice, you need to weigh if it were easier to just get a part time job working somewhere until you are more comfortable for starting up a new business. Better yet get a part time job if you can in the industry that you want to try to get your own business with.

****

Times You Might Need To File With a Sch C

What are the times that you might need to file with a Schedule C that you might normally not think of? That is a very good question.

Sometimes it isn't obvious until you get a letter back from the IRS asking why you aren't including some types of income (or they were filed incorrectly on Line 21 of your 1040).

If you have any children (you know, dependents, those creatures that lay around most of the year playing video games and eating you out of house and home, right?) who take a part time job over the summer and they get a 1099 instead of a W2, they need to file a Schedule C.

Be aware that just because you (or your kids) also didn't receive a 1099, if it is less than $600 it doesn't automatically mean you don't have to show it as income. The business may still report that they paid your kid and for whatever reason accidentally not send him a 1099. Or maybe the company the kid worked for is flakey. That happens all the time.

You are taxed on all world-wide income generally speaking here in the United States that you earn. State taxing authorities may follow suit as well.

How about if your main compensation is wage income earned as an employee and is reported to you on a Form W-2, but you worked a temporary job as a self-employed independent contractor and your compensation was reported to them on a Form 1099-MISC, box 7? Yes, you need to report this on a Schedule C.

How about you buy and sell gold in your living room? How about you sell Avon or any kind of products from your home? You are effectively operating what is called a direct sales business. Direct sellers re-sell products, often using the house party strategy. You need to use a Schedule C.

What if you are in the situation that some teenagers are in? Self-employed and receive little to no wage income. If you perform services for other companies, for which you are paid over $600, you should also receive a Form 1099-MISC. You may also have income from individuals who are not required to issue reporting forms. In this case, it's your responsibility to track their income as I stated earlier. You might have heard the expression "statutory employee". Statutory employees generally file a Schedule C. Who is considered a statutory employee?

a. An officer of a corporation who does not perform any services or performs only minor services and who neither receives nor is entitled to receive, directly or indirectly, any remuneration.

b. A full-time traveling or city salesperson who solicits orders from wholesalers, restaurants, or similar establishments on behalf of a principal. The merchandise sold must be for resale or for supplies used in the buyer's business.

c. A full-time life insurance agent whose principal business activity is selling life insurance and/or annuity contracts for one life insurance company.

d. An agent-driver or commission-driver engaged in distributing meat, vegetables, bakery goods, beverages (other than milk), or laundry or dry cleaning services.

e. A home worker performing work on material or goods furnished by the employer.

Statutory employees do NOT receive a Form 1099-MISC, but receive a Form W-2 with the box 13, "Statutory Employee," box marked. They report their wages and allowable expenses on Schedule C, but they do not pay SE tax because their employer already withheld for social security and Medicare taxes.

Self Employment Tax Sucks But You Have To Pay It

Not only do sole proprietors need to pay income tax on their business net profit, they need to pay self-employment tax (SE tax), which is the equivalent of social security and Medicare taxes. The tax rate as of the 2010 edition of this book is 15.3% (12.4% for social security and 2.9% for Medicare), representing both the employee and employer contribution, on 92.35% of their net income from self-employment. The tax is added on the Form 1040 as an additional tax after figuring income tax. However, you are also eligible to deduct one-half of their contribution as an adjustment to income.

Statutory employees do not pay SE tax because their employers must treat them as employees for social security and Medicare tax purposes and withhold these taxes from their wages. Don't you love tax law complexity?

Certain of you ladies and gentlemen out there are exempt from paying SE tax:

If you are the executor or administrator of an estate, unless you are a professional fiduciary or works for a business held by the estate you are off the hook.

If you are part of the dying breed of newspaper carriers you might be exempt in some cases.

If you are a notary public you may not have to pay self employment taxes.

If you are clergy who have applied to and received approval from the IRS because of conscientious objection to public insurance due to religious belief you may be off the hook as well. My suggestion is don't try to scam the IRS, they have seen it all and are pretty sophisticated these days in figuring out if you owe self employment tax or not.

The Schedule C Walk Thru

I already here you yelling at me, "Hey, Kim, what do we need a walk thru for the Schedule C since tax software all over the place will fill out the forms for me auto-magically?"

The answer is that the software works on a very basic level and is only as good as the person that is entering it. As shocking as it may seem, some people fill out tax forms incorrectly. Some people even try to change numbers to fit what they want to see instead of what actually happened with their business. Can you believe that? Wow.

Okay, I will go through everything pretty clearly for you with what you can and cannot do and then you are on your own. Fair enough?

Rock on!

If you want to follow along, you can download from www.irs.gov the form, Schedule C (Form 1040). Please make sure it is for the most recent year that you can find for tax filing and the respective instructions.

For now, as of the printing of this edition of the book, the form isn't changing dramatically. A sample of a Schedule C is on the next page.

I'll wait till you want to continue. Ready?

Let's go.

Everything that is above the part of the form that says "Part I" is considered the "HEADING".

Here is how you fill out the heading for your business. Let's fill out the "Name of Proprietor". Enter your name. Then enter your social security for the Social Security part on the first line. If you are using software from a box or Internet, make sure you can view the form and that whatever you entered is flowing through.

****

BUSINESS FASHION TIP:

Before you start your business, make sure that you have your accounting software, spreadsheet or documents set up for the categories that you need.

As you purchase products, spend money for contractors, buy raw materials for your products, make sure that you keep your bookkeeping current so when you print out your income statements they will reflect what you've been doing. It will make income tax preparation easier as well.

****

SCHEDULE C (Form 1040)

Department of the Treasury Internal Revenue Service (99)

Profit or Loss From Business

(Sole Proprietorship)

▶ Partnerships, joint ventures, etc., generally must file Form 1065 or 1065-B.
▶ Attach to Form 1040, 1040NR, or 1041. ▶ See Instructions for Schedule C (Form 1040).

OMB No. 1545-0074

2010

Attachment Sequence No. 09

Name of proprietor | Social security number (SSN)

A Principal business or profession, including product or service (see instructions) | B Enter code from pages C-9, 10, & 11 ▶

C Business name. If no separate business name, leave blank. | D Employer ID number (EIN), if any

E Business address (including suite or room no.) ▶
City, town or post office, state, and ZIP code

F Accounting method: (1) ☐ Cash (2) ☐ Accrual (3) ☐ Other (specify) ▶

G Did you "materially participate" in the operation of this business during 2010? If "No," see instructions for limit on losses ☐ Yes ☐ No

H If you started or acquired this business during 2010, check here ▶ ☐

Part I Income

1	Gross receipts or sales. Caution. See instructions and check the box if: • This income was reported to you on Form W-2 and the "Statutory employee" box on that form was checked, or • You are a member of a qualified joint venture reporting only rental real estate income not subject to self-employment tax. Also see instructions for limit on losses. ▶ ☐	1	
2	Returns and allowances	2	
3	Subtract line 2 from line 1	3	
4	Cost of goods sold (from line 42 on page 2)	4	
5	**Gross profit.** Subtract line 4 from line 3	5	
6	Other income, including federal and state gasoline or fuel tax credit or refund (see instructions)	6	
7	**Gross income.** Add lines 5 and 6 ▶	7	

Part II Expenses. Enter expenses for business use of your home **only** on line 30.

8	Advertising	8		18	Office expense	18	
9	Car and truck expenses (see instructions)	9		19	Pension and profit-sharing plans	19	
10	Commissions and fees	10		20	Rent or lease (see instructions):		
11	Contract labor (see instructions)	11		a	Vehicles, machinery, and equipment	20a	
12	Depletion	12		b	Other business property	20b	
13	Depreciation and section 179 expense deduction (not included in Part III) (see instructions)	13		21	Repairs and maintenance	21	
				22	Supplies (not included in Part III)	22	
				23	Taxes and licenses	23	
				24	Travel, meals, and entertainment:		
				a	Travel	24a	
14	Employee benefit programs (other than on line 19)	14		b	Deductible meals and entertainment (see instructions)	24b	
15	Insurance (other than health)	15		25	Utilities	25	
16	Interest:			26	Wages (less employment credits)	26	
a	Mortgage (paid to banks, etc.)	16a		27	Other expenses (from line 48 on page 2)	27	
b	Other	16b					
17	Legal and professional services	17					

28	**Total expenses** before expenses for business use of home. Add lines 8 through 27 ▶	28	
29	Tentative profit or (loss). Subtract line 28 from line 7	29	
30	Expenses for business use of your home. Attach Form 8829	30	
31	**Net profit or (loss).** Subtract line 30 from line 29. • If a profit, enter on both **Form 1040, line 12,** and **Schedule SE, line 2,** or on **Form 1040NR, line 13** (if you checked the box on line 1, see instructions). Estates and trusts, enter on **Form 1041, line 3.** • If a loss, you **must** go to line 32.	31	
32	If you have a loss, check the box that describes your investment in this activity (see instructions). • If you checked 32a, enter the loss on both **Form 1040, line 12,** and **Schedule SE, line 2,** or on **Form 1040NR, line 13** (if you checked the box on line 1, see the line 31 instructions). Estates and trusts, enter on **Form 1041, line 3.** • If you checked 32b, you **must** attach Form 6198. Your loss may be limited.	32a ☐ All investment is at risk. 32b ☐ Some investment is not at risk.	

For Paperwork Reduction Act Notice, see your tax return instructions. Cat. No. 11334P **Schedule C (Form 1040) 2010**

For Box A, you will need to enter your business or profession and then what is the product or service that you are selling. For example, if you own a barber shop. You would put BARBER SHOP/HAIRCUTS as your entry.

For Box B you will need to enter the **Principal Business or Professional Activity Code** that applies to your business. There are a lot of categories but there may not be one specifically for your business so you may want to get it as close as possible. The reason? The IRS compares your business to others in the same category and looks for reasonableness. It pays to take some time to get the category right. You can find the categories on the instructions for Schedule C Profit or Loss from Business and using the 2010 edition let us take a snapshot of one page that might have what we are looking for.

****

BUSINESS FASHION TIP:

Check with other people who are in the same business that you are planning to go into and see what professional activity code that they use.

Make sure though before you do that they haven't had problems with the IRS or state government agencies for using the incorrect professional activity code or other things that you generally don't want to have anything to do with. In short, don't take advice from people who are in trouble with the IRS.

****

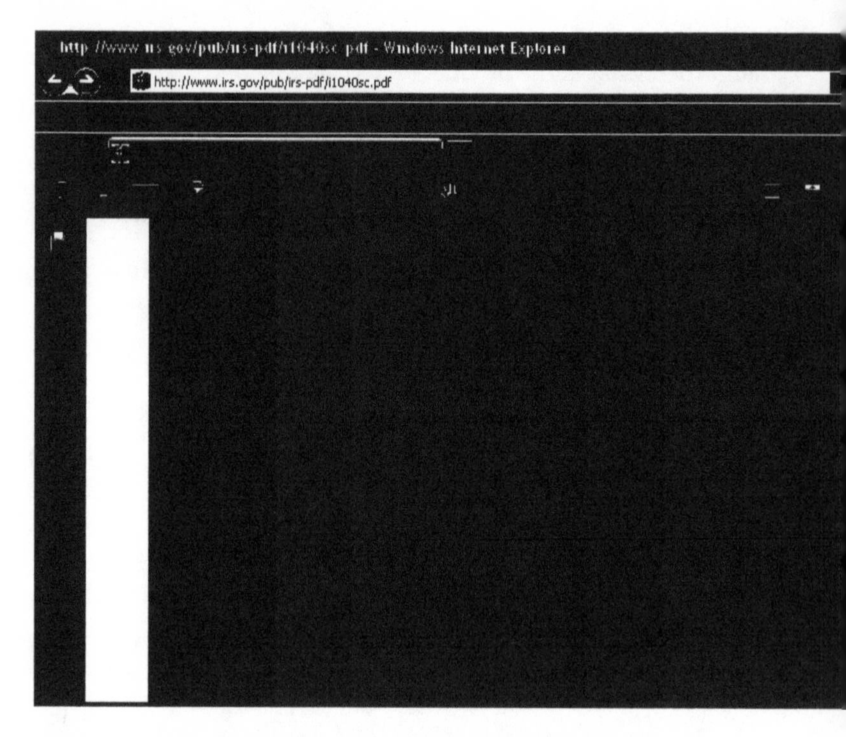

Take a look in the third column under “Other Services”. There is the code for Barber Shop so we will use 812111.

Moving down to Line C we enter the name if it is different than the name that we are filing the tax return under. Let us pretend that we are doing business as (DBA) “Super Styling Haircuts”. By the way for most DBAs you need to file and pay a fee with your local city or state authorities. Check your local area and the Internet for filing DBAs near you. The process is generally straight forward and it allows you to open a bank account with your business name.

On Line D we enter our Employer ID Number (EIN) which you can get from the IRS website. You only need this if you are planning on hiring other people to work for you or if you plan on using a lot of sub contracting. The Employer ID Number (EIN) gets used instead of your social security number for reporting and keeps access to having to share your social security number for reporting at a minimum.

If you don't have an EIN number and don't need it, you can leave this box blank.

Line or Box E is for your address. Please do not use a Post Office or P.O. box number. If you need to, use your home address. The IRS does not like to see post office boxes as business addresses.
There should be for Box F, the type of Accounting Method you are using. There are three types – cash, accrual and hybrid. Of the three, naturally, cash tends to be the most common for most sole proprietorships.

Remember if you are just starting up your business to think this through because whatever method you are using, you will be using it going forward without changing it. If you do have to change it, the IRS (and respective state agencies) will want to know why.

The three methods are:

1. Cash method - Only income and expenses actually or constructively received or paid during the year are reported. Income is constructively received when it is credited to your account or set aside for your use.
2. Accrual method - Inventories are usually required for clients who produce, purchase, or sell merchandise. Most of these business people use the accrual method. Under this method, income is recorded as sales and charges are incurred, regardless if payment is actually received. For example, when the business sells an item in 2010, but receives payment in 2011, the income is reported as 2010 income. Likewise,

expenses are reported as they are incurred, not as they are paid.
3. Other, hybrid method - This combines the cash and accrual methods.

Sales and inventory are reported using the accrual method.

All other items of income and expenses use the cash method.

Okay? So for the barber business we would use the CASH method for our example.

Boxes G and H need to be answered. The questions are "Did you materially participate in the business?" and "Did you start the business last year?"

A person materially participates when they are involved in the business in a regular, continuous, and substantial way. If the proprietor does not materially participate, any loss from the business is considered
a passive loss.

Passive losses can only be deducted if there is passive income in the same year. If you aren't sure about this, take a minute to please re-read the above statements. They are very important to understand.

A sole proprietor materially participates in a business if one of seven tests is met:

1. Worked more than 500 hours during the tax year.

2. Participates more than anyone else.

3. Participated more than 100 hours, and no one else participates more.

4. Activity is a significant participation activity, and participation exceeds 500 hours during the year.
5. There has been participation for any five of the previous ten years.

6. The activity is a personal service activity in which the taxpayer has materially participated for any three preceding tax years.

7. Based on the facts, there is participation in the activity on a regular, continuous, and substantial basis for more than 100 hours.

The Schedule C instructions contain more details and that can be found on the IRS website. A problem I find sometimes is with confused taxpayers who think fail to disclose to me that they worked over the summer (example: with a movie production company) and received a 1099 for the $4900 he made. I ask everybody if they had any W-2 or contract income (1099). I ask them repeatedly. The people sometimes say "no".

Guess what? The client gets a computer audit letter stating that they failed to declare income. When I talk to the client they are in "shock". Hey, they didn't tell me after I asked several times if they had any other income. Did they think the production company wasn't going to show them as an expense as a contractor? Really?

Save yourself the grief and get into the habit of living with full disclosure. You aren't hiding anything from anybody.

If you have any questions or doubts, always refer back to the source reference material besides this book: the IRS and respective state agencies. They update their information as soon as tax law changes and they can give you guidance as to what they are looking for on their forms. For more specific questions or experiences, please consult a tax professional.

Sch C Income

Here we come to the fun part of the Schedule C. Listing your income.

How do you do that?

If it came from a 1099, you should list off who it came from and how much. Some software packages prompt you for this information. For the Schedule C, Line 1 you put in your total gross receipts and/or self employment income.

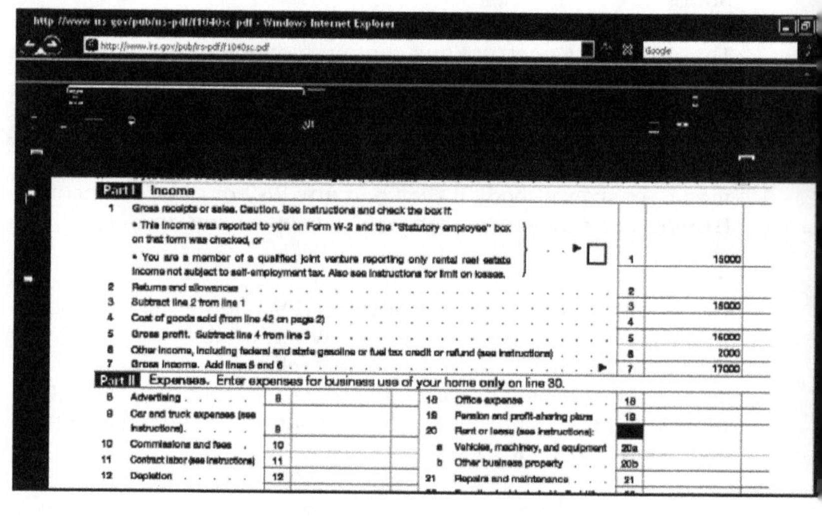

http://www.irs.gov/pub/irs-pdf/f1040sc.pdf - Windows Internet Explorer

Part I Income

1	Gross receipts or sales. Caution. See instructions and check the box if: • This income was reported to you on Form W-2 and the "Statutory employee" box on that form was checked, or • You are a member of a qualified joint venture reporting only rental real estate income not subject to self-employment tax. Also see instructions for limit on losses. ▶ ☐	1	15000
2	Returns and allowances	2	
3	Subtract line 2 from line 1	3	15000
4	Cost of goods sold (from line 42 on page 2)	4	
5	Gross profit. Subtract line 4 from line 3	5	15000
6	Other income, including federal and state gasoline or fuel tax credit or refund (see instructions)	6	2000
7	Gross income. Add lines 5 and 6 ▶	7	17000

Part II Expenses. Enter expenses for business use of your home only on line 30.

8	Advertising	8		18	Office expense	18	
9	Car and truck expenses (see instructions)	9		19	Pension and profit-sharing plans	19	
				20	Rent or lease (see instructions):		
10	Commissions and fees	10		a	Vehicles, machinery, and equipment	20a	
11	Contract labor (see instructions)	11		b	Other business property	20b	
12	Depletion	12		21	Repairs and maintenance	21	

So let us say that you made $15,000 from haircuts last year and then you also made $2000 in other income. Your barber shop won $2000 for the Best Hair Cut in the City contest. Congrats! It will help generate word of mouth interest in your shop and you made some extra cash.

The downside is you need to declare it as income. No problems though because you don't mind paying taxes if your income goes up because that shows that you are making money (a fact that a lot of people tend to forget).

Some other items that might be considered as "Other Income" besides prize and contest cash in connection to your business are recovered bad debt (but only if you had previously deducted it as an expense), interest received on notes and accounts receivables (and not to be confused with Schedule B interest you get from banks, etc).

Other forms of other income are Federal or state fuel tax credits or refunds, income from scrap sales, recapture of excessive depreciation from Section 179 if use of listed property drops below 50%. That is a little out of scope for this book but you can find out more from the IRS website if you are curious.

Did you notice a line item for Cost of Goods sold? That comes from PART III of our Schedule C on the next page. If you are involved in a business that manufactures or carries an inventory you will need to fill out this section.

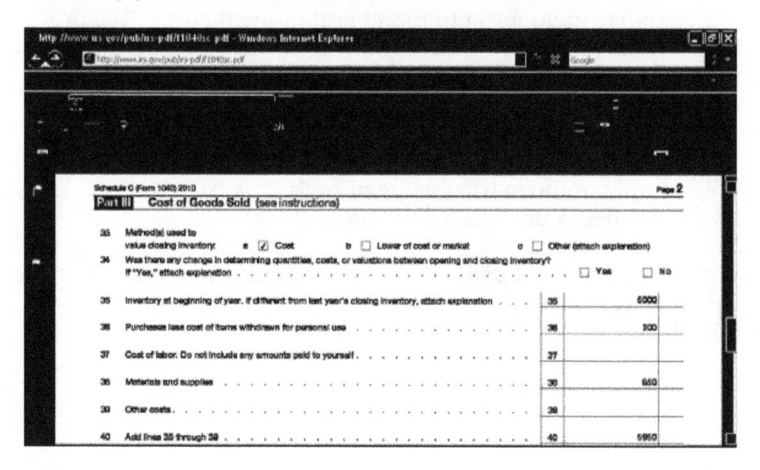

Schedule C (Form 1040) 2013 Page 2

Part III Cost of Goods Sold (see instructions)

33 Method(s) used to value closing inventory: a ☑ Cost b ☐ Lower of cost or market c ☐ Other (attach explanation)

34 Was there any change in determining quantities, costs, or valuations between opening and closing inventory? If "Yes," attach explanation ☐ Yes ☐ No

35	Inventory at beginning of year. If different from last year's closing inventory, attach explanation	35	5000
36	Purchases less cost of items withdrawn for personal use	36	300
37	Cost of labor. Do not include any amounts paid to yourself	37	
38	Materials and supplies	38	650
39	Other costs	39	
40	Add lines 35 through 39	40	5950

Let us pretend that the barber shop also has soaps, shampoos, combs and razors it sells. Cost of goods sold is the expense a business incurs to produce or sell its products.

To calculate cost of goods sold, start with the beginning inventory and add the amounts for direct purchases, direct labor costs, and overhead costs. From the total, subtract withdrawals for personal use and ending inventory. The first thing we need to recognize is the method that we value the inventory at. The three methods are: cost, lower of cost or market and "other".

Most inventory methods tend to be cost or lower of cost/market. If you are using another method or valuation you need to attach a statement with your tax return when you file it to let the IRS know.

Cost Method
Under this method, goods are valued at their invoice price. You then add shipping charges to the invoice price. Discounts, on the other hand, are subtracted. The cost value of merchandise includes both direct and indirect costs. Goods that were inventoried at the beginning of the year and that still remain at the end of the year should be valued as they were at the beginning.

Lower of Cost or Market
This compares the market value of each item with its cost. The lower number is used for valuation.

Inventory is tracked using different methods though the most common are called first-in first-out (FIFO) and last-in first-out (LIFO).

In the first-in first-out (FIFO) method, the first goods purchased or produced are the first sold. Either inventory valuation method can be used with FIFO. The last-in first-out (LIFO) method is different. This option considers the last goods purchased or produced to be the first sold. LIFO requires the cost method of inventory valuation to be used.

Important note: You cannot arbitrarily change accounting methods from one year to the next because it makes your numbers look better. You can change your method of valuation but you need to demonstrate a track record with it to show that you are treating your business accounting properly.

Beginning Inventory

Inventory at the beginning of one year is usually the same as the ending inventory from the previous year.

In the case of a retailer, for example, any merchandise on hand when the store closes December 31 should be in stock when the store opens January 1. If there is a difference, attach an explanation to the return.

****

BUSINESS FASHION TIP:

Don't change nest year's starting inventory counts after you reported the ending inventory already. They should be the same right? The IRS will raise a computer generated eyebrow at you.

****

Beginning inventory includes:
1. For manufacturers, the total value of raw materials, work in process, finished goods, and materials and supplies.
2. For merchants, the cost of merchandise to be sold.

That's it for that.

Charitable Donations

What do you do with gifts to charity? You reduce the beginning inventory when donating inventory items to charity. This ensures that the cost of goods sold is accurate.

If deductions are itemized, the inventory value of the donation may be deductible on Schedule A. Do not confuse inventory value with fair market value, however. When tallying the deduction, you must use the inventory value.

Taxpayers can deduct costs for donated property as cost of goods sold.

This must be done in the year of contribution. In such a scenario, the Schedule A deduction is not allowed.

Examples: Pretend that I am the barber and I also sell shampoo as part of my living. In 2010, I donated some shampoo to a church/synagogue or mosque. The hair shampoo, valued at $100, was purchased and inventoried in 2009. When I donated the hair shampoo, the Fair Market Value (FMV) was $200. I would reduce my 2010 beginning inventory of hair products by $100. I can also claim a $100 deduction on his Schedule A. Notice that I am not claiming the FMV here, right?

Pretend that the situation is different now. Let me, as Barber Hair Stylist Kim, donate $200 worth of hair products. This time I purchased them in 2010, the year of the donation. My cost of goods includes the $200 worth of shampoo that I bought this year. I cannot claim the Schedule A deduction if I am itemizing.

With me? Good.

If you are having a hard time, don't be embarrassed to go back and read sections several times. There is no shame in that. I do it myself on parts of tax law that I don't understand.

Purchases

The purchase amount includes any sales tax and shipping. Any discounts must be excluded. Purchase amounts include:

For manufacturers, the cost of raw materials or parts used to manufacture finished products.

For merchants, all merchandise bought for resale. If business merchandise is used for personal use, subtract the merchandise cost from the purchase cost.

Example: Kim sells Avon. He paid $1,750 for products during the year. Additionally, He paid $52 in shipping costs and received a $38 prompt-payment discount. Kim appropriated $67 worth of products for personal use. The amount of Kim's purchases is $3,697.

[$1,750 + $52 – $38 – $67 = $1,697]

Cost of Labor

Work that prepares a product for sale is a labor cost. Manufacturing and mining businesses usually include labor costs in cost of goods sold. Merchants, conversely, usually cannot.

Materials and Supplies

This includes hardware and chemicals used in the manufacturing process.

Other Costs

Other costs are amounts spent on:

a. Containers and packages essential to the product. If not essential, the costs are counted as operating expenses.

b. Freight-in, express-in, and cartage-in for raw materials, supplies used in production, and merchandise purchased for sale. (Freight out, express-out, and cartage-out are operating expenses, not cost of goods sold.)

c. Overhead expenses, such as equipment depreciation, heat, insurance, light, labor, power, rent, supervision, and taxes that are direct and necessary manufacturing expenses.

Ending Inventory

This is inventory on hand at the end of the year. Proprietors should take a physical inventory at the end of each accounting period.

Cost of Goods Sold

To calculate cost of goods sold, add beginning inventory, purchases, and other cost of goods, and then subtract ending inventory. For expenses with both cost of goods sold and operating expenses, divide them and claim the proper amount for each.

Exception to Inventory

The cash method of accounting can be used if a principal business test and an annual gross receipts test is met. When doing so, inventory items must be counted as incidental materials and supplies.

A principal business should meet one of the following tests:

a. Business does not have a North American Industry Classification System (NAICS) code.

b. Ineligible businesses include: mining, manufacturing, publishing, wholesale trades, and certain retail trades.

c. The services supplied by the business are incidental to the business.

d. Business fabricates or modifies personal property according to customer specifications.

Taxpayers can meet the average annual gross receipts test in one of the following ways:

1. Receipts total $1 million or less for each tax year after December 17, 1999.
2. The average annual gross receipts total $10 million or less for each of the previous three years.

The item costs are deductible either in the year of sale or the year they are paid for, whichever is later. For more information on these rules, see IRS Publication 538, Accounting Periods and Methods.

At this point you may be wondering why should you care about such high dollar values and thresholds. Depending on the business you are getting into, you may not net a lot of money but the gross amount of your receipts (especially with inflation in certain things) can result in receipts over one million dollars.

Better to have the information tucked away somewhere even if you aren't going to use it just quite yet.

Sch C Expenses

Now we come to the part that tends to get abused a lot but is actually very important in running your business. Expenses.

Let's take a look once again at the Schedule C. This time we will be looking at Part II which is the expenses section.

This is the place that most people mess up one way or another when they end up doing their income taxes (based on my experience with hundreds of tax returns).

People either don't realize they can take legitimate expenses for their businesses or they go nuts trying to expense everything they can think of and I usually get them mad at me by telling them that they can't deduct certain things (like commuting miles).

Let us go through the categories and take a look at what can be taken as expenses keeping in mind it has to be relevant and an actual expense for your business. There are plenty of legitimate expenses that you can take no matter what business you are in. In fact, for purposes of the Earned Income Tax Credit, there is also a red flag if you don't take any expenses on your Schedule C.

If you are entitled to take legit expenses for your sole proprietorship, then take them.

SCHEDULE C (Form 1040)

Department of the Treasury Internal Revenue Service (99)

Profit or Loss From Business

(Sole Proprietorship)

▶ Partnerships, joint ventures, etc., generally must file Form 1065 or 1065-B.
▶ Attach to Form 1040, 1040NR, or 1041. ▶ See Instructions for Schedule C (Form 1040).

OMB No. 1545-0074

2010

Attachment Sequence No. 09

Name of proprietor | Social security number (SSN)

A Principal business or profession, including product or service (see instructions) | B Enter code from pages C-9, 10, & 11 ▶

C Business name. If no separate business name, leave blank. | D Employer ID number (EIN), if any

E Business address (including suite or room no.) ▶

City, town or post office, state, and ZIP code

F Accounting method: (1) ☐ Cash (2) ☐ Accrual (3) ☐ Other (specify) ▶

G Did you "materially participate" in the operation of this business during 2010? If "No," see instructions for limit on losses ☐ Yes ☐ No

H If you started or acquired this business during 2010, check here . . . ▶ ☐

Part I Income

1	Gross receipts or sales. Caution. See instructions and check the box if: • This income was reported to you on Form W-2 and the "Statutory employee" box on that form was checked, or • You are a member of a qualified joint venture reporting only rental real estate income not subject to self-employment tax. Also see instructions for limit on losses. . . . ▶ ☐	1	
2	Returns and allowances	2	
3	Subtract line 2 from line 1	3	
4	Cost of goods sold (from line 42 on page 2)	4	
5	Gross profit. Subtract line 4 from line 3	5	
6	Other income, including federal and state gasoline or fuel tax credit or refund (see instructions)	6	
7	Gross income. Add lines 5 and 6 ▶	7	

Part II Expenses. Enter expenses for business use of your home only on line 30.

8	Advertising	8		18	Office expense	18	
9	Car and truck expenses (see instructions)	9		19	Pension and profit-sharing plans	19	
10	Commissions and fees	10		20	Rent or lease (see instructions):		
11	Contract labor (see instructions)	11		a	Vehicles, machinery, and equipment	20a	
12	Depletion	12		b	Other business property	20b	
13	Depreciation and section 179 expense deduction (not included in Part III) (see instructions)	13		21	Repairs and maintenance	21	
				22	Supplies (not included in Part III)	22	
				23	Taxes and licenses	23	
				24	Travel, meals, and entertainment:		
				a	Travel	24a	
14	Employee benefit programs (other than on line 19)	14		b	Deductible meals and entertainment (see instructions)	24b	
15	Insurance (other than health)	15		25	Utilities	25	
16	Interest:			26	Wages (less employment credits)	26	
a	Mortgage (paid to banks, etc.)	16a		27	Other expenses (from line 48 on page 2)	27	
b	Other	16b					
17	Legal and professional services	17					

28	Total expenses before expenses for business use of home. Add lines 8 through 27 ▶	28	
29	Tentative profit or (loss). Subtract line 28 from line 7	29	
30	Expenses for business use of your home. Attach Form 8829	30	
31	Net profit or (loss). Subtract line 30 from line 29. • If a profit, enter on both Form 1040, line 12, and Schedule SE, line 2, or on Form 1040NR, line 13 (if you checked the box on line 1, see instructions). Estates and trusts, enter on Form 1041, line 3. • If a loss, you must go to line 32.	31	

32 If you have a loss, check the box that describes your investment in this activity (see instructions).

• If you checked 32a, enter the loss on both Form 1040, line 12, and Schedule SE, line 2, or on Form 1040NR, line 13 (if you checked the box on line 1, see the line 31 instructions). Estates and trusts, enter on Form 1041, line 3.

• If you checked 32b, you must attach Form 6198. Your loss may be limited.

32a ☐ All investment is at risk.
32b ☐ Some investment is not at risk.

For Paperwork Reduction Act Notice, see your tax return instructions. Cat. No. 11334P Schedule C (Form 1040) 2010

Here are the expenses by category and what is generally acceptable for each one (depending on if it is relevant to your business):

Advertising

Expenses that are used to promote your business would go here. For my barber shop that might be newspaper ads (anybody read the papers anymore?), flyers (generally a bad marketing investment unless you get a great rate since that includes the cost of distributing them), television and radio promotions (good), Internet banners (depends if you have good web locations) and business cards.

Depending on your business you may have more or less advertising expenses. Make sure you save your receipts and bank statements.

Car and Truck Expenses

Car and truck expenses incurred for business purposes for your tax home
go here. Two items which would NOT go here are car depreciation (that would go on Line 13 for the 2010 Schedule C) and lease payments which would go Line 20 a – vehicles rented.

The IRS allows you two flavors of deductions and you can only use one of them at a time. You cannot use both.
You either use the actual expenses or the optional standard mileage rate method.

When you first put your vehicle in service, you make the decision as to what you want to take – actual expenses or the standard mileage rate.

In either case, you need to know the cost of your vehicle, description, date you placed it in service for your business, total miles you drove in the year, the total business miles and the amount of commuting miles. Keep track of this information on a spreadsheet as a back-up in case you change tax professionals or the back up on your software from the website goes away. It does happen.

Commissions and Fees

If there are any fees or amounts that you paid for services that were not included on any other line of Schedule C, you deduct them under this section.

Er, remember that they have to be related to your work.

Contract Labor

If you pay anybody who isn't an employee, such as a contractor or subcontractor, you put the amounts for their services here. If you hired and paid anybody more than $600 you need to issue them 1099-MISC forms. For more information visit the IRS website or contact your tax pro on this.

Depletion

Do you own any oil wells? Any gas wells? How about that gold ore in your backyard? Any timber on your land that you are chopping down and selling, you mad axe person, you? No?

Then depletion probably doesn't apply to your business. The only things you can deplete are the items above that cannot be replenished and own a finite amount of (oil, gas, mineral rights and timber). Land, as you may or may not remember, cannot be created nor destroyed (despite earthquakes) in the eyes of tax law and therefore doesn't apply.

Depreciation

Depreciation is an income tax deduction that allows a taxpayer to recover the cost or other basis of certain property. It is an annual allowance for the wear and tear, deterioration, or obsolescence of the property.

Most types of tangible property (except, land), such as buildings, machinery, vehicles, furniture, and equipment are depreciable. Likewise, certain intangible property, such as patents, copyrights, and computer software is depreciable.

In some years, you have been allowed to deduct the entire value of tangible property up to certain limits. You need to check with the particular year you are filing a tax return for to see if anything like that applies to you in your current situation. By the way even though it may seem obvious, once an item has been reduced to a zero dollar value, there is nothing left to depreciate on it.

Hang onto tax returns that have depreciable property still being depreciated on them. This is especially true if you have rental property that you expect to hold onto for a long time. If you want to play it safe,
scan and save the info as pdf, Word or electronic documents (especially work sheets to support financial positions).

In order for a taxpayer to be allowed a depreciation deduction for a property, the property must meet all the following requirements:

1. The taxpayer must own the property. Taxpayers may also depreciate any capital improvements for property the taxpayer leases.
2. A taxpayer must use the property in business or in an income-producing activity. If a taxpayer uses a property for

business and for personal purposes, the taxpayer can only deduct depreciation based only on the business use of that property.
3. The property must have a determinable useful life of more than one year.

Pretty straight forward stuff so far, huh? There is some more that you need to be aware of.

It is important that you get the property class information right and the methods that are being used for depreciation. Even if a taxpayer meets the preceding requirements for a property, a taxpayer cannot depreciate the following property:

1. Property placed in service and disposed of in same year.
2. Equipment used to build capital improvements. A taxpayer must add otherwise allowable depreciation on the equipment during the period of construction to the basis of the improvements.
3. Certain term interests.

Depreciation begins when a taxpayer places property in service for use in a trade or business or for the production of income. You will need the start date for when you placed the property in service and the cost of the property. The property ceases to be depreciable when the taxpayer has fully recovered the property's cost or other basis or when the taxpayer retires it from service, whichever happens first.

A taxpayer must identify several items to ensure the proper depreciation of a property, including:

1. The depreciation method for the property
2. The class life of the asset
3. Whether the property is "Listed Property"
4. Whether the taxpayer elects to expense any portion of the asset
5. Whether the taxpayer qualifies for any "bonus" first year depreciation

6. The depreciable basis of the property

The Modified Accelerated Cost Recovery System (MACRS) is the proper depreciation method for most property. Additional information about MACRS, and the other components of depreciation are in Publication 946, How to Depreciate Property available from our good friends at the IRS at www.irs.gov.

A taxpayer must use Form 4562, Depreciation and Amortization, to report depreciation on a tax return. Form 4562 is divided into six sections and the Instructions for Form 4562 contain information on how, and when to fill out each section. You may also find information on this at the IRS website as well.

Employee Benefit Programs

Are you a kind and generous boss who is contributing to his employees' programs? If you are contributing to an employee fringe benefit program, the amounts are deductible. Included in the fringe benefit program are amounts you contributed to education, recreation, health, dependent care, and adoption assistance.

Most start up businesses have enough time keeping solvent their first years and if you can afford to help your employees – good for you and please teach the rest of us how you are doing it!

If you have contractors please make sure that you are generating 1099s for them as well.

Insurance (Other Than Health)

Please make a note of this and if need be tattoo it somewhere:

Insurance Payments can only be deducted in the year they apply. It doesn't matter if you are cash or an accrual accounting method.

If you are prepaying three years of theft insurance because you are getting a great rate you can only take one year's worth of payments for the year that it is applicable to. That is it.

Premiums that you pay for protecting your business against loss (say theft insurance) are deductible as an operating expense.
Some other types of insurance premiums that may be applicable to your business include fire, theft, flood, merchandise, inventory, credit, worker's compensation, business interruption (good to have if power goes out), errors and omissions, disability (for employees), malpractice, and product liability.
Interest

Interest expense deductions on our Schedule C come in two flavors:

Mortgage Interest (Paid to Banks, etc)
And
Other Interest

Mortgage Interest (Paid to Banks, etc) is where you deduct the interest portion of mortgage payments made to financial institutions on real property used in the business and for which you received a Form 1098 for. If you are working out of your home, the qualified business portions of all home offices are computed on a special form (Form 8829).

Other Interest is interest paid on business indebtedness other than mortgage interest. This includes financial charges on business loans and credit card purchases. Any interest (including mortgage interest) is deductible only in the year that it applies.

Legal and Professional Services

This is one of Kim's favorite categories to review with a client. Expenses paid for an attorney, accountants and any other professional fees that are ordinary and necessary to conduct business. Expenses for the preparation of tax forms related to business get placed here. (As a tax professional that is why this is one of my favorite categories – My services aren't treated as a free lunch).

Office Expense

Offices expenses are what we would call "consumable" meaning that you need to replenish them from time to time. Think of things like pads, pens and pencils, order or receipt books, stickies, computer and printer supplies, calculators, cash registers, copy machines, stamps, overnight delivery charges, registered or certified mail expenses, rental of a postage meter, postal box, etc. You get the idea.

Pension and Profit-Sharing Plans

If you are making contributions to a pension, profit-sharing, or annuity plan for employees, you would take the deduction here. If the plan includes the sole proprietor, the amount contributed for you as sole prop can only be deducted as an adjustment on Form 1040.

For more information on this please check with the IRS website. Most start ups barely have cash for their business leave alone setting up their pension or profit sharing plans.

Rent or Lease

Renting or leasing comes in two flavors for this category:

Vehicles, Machinery, & Equipment
-and-
Other Business Property

This is another two line deal similar to other items that we have covered. If you are renting vehicles or equipment, like a truck and maybe a floor polishing machine you can use this category if it fits for your rental of the equipment.

Rental or lease payments for real property (like your office) would go under Other Business Property.

Repairs and Maintenance

If you are spending money for anything that is needed to maintain business property in an ordinary, efficient operating condition it may be deductible, depending on your business. The cost of repairs includes labor, supplies, the annual portion of the cost of service contracts and other items incidental to the repair.

You cannot deduct your time, your labor and the time of your relatives and friends if they are helping out, sorry.

If you incur a capital expenditure that increases the value of an asset, increases the productivity of the asset, prolongs the useful life or adapts it for another use, you have to depreciate it.

Supplies

Any supplies not included in Part III of our Schedule C that are necessary to your business are deductible. Make sure they are reasonable for the type of business you are in.

Example: Bullet reloading supplies are not applicable for a daycare center though they might be applicable for a shooting range.

Taxes and Licenses

Any taxes that you pay that are attributable to the trade or business are deductible. Some of the taxes that might apply are:

1. Real estate and personal property taxes.
2. State and local taxes.
3. Payroll taxes that you pay on behalf of your employees.
4. Sales taxes imposed on the seller of goods and services.
   NOTE: If you are passing these on to your customers, make sure you include them in your gross receipts. Thanks!
5. Licenses such as occupational, chauffeur, building, State Bar Association, etc and any regulatory fees paid annually to state and local governments in connection with your gig are deducted here.

Travel, Meals and Entertainment

The limits that you can take are determined each year and are the same for employees and the self employed. Travel expenses include airfare, cab fare, bus fare, etc that have been made outside your tax home. Meal and entertainment expenses must be for a clear business purpose and substantial business discussions held before or after the event.

If you aren't already keeping a business log, it is time to start. Keep track of the date, time, who you met with, purpose of the meal, etc. If you want to buy a log book please check out my book, *The Greenblatt Business Expense and Mileage Logbook* available from Amazon and my website.

Utilities

Can you allocate between your non-business personal use of utilities and your business use? If you can, you can deduct the cost of heat, lights, power, telephone and Internet access. If you have separate utility meters for your business office – that is the way to go if you can. If not, make sure you allocate.

Some warnings that I give to my clients:

No portion of the base rate for your first telephone is deductible. If you add a second line for business purposes or extra services, such as call waiting for business, the business portion is deductible. Long distance charges for business purposes are deductible.

You also cannot take the monthly basic cost of cell phones used personally and for business. The cost is not deductible similar to a first landline. Only charges for additional cell phone features that are business related are deductible. Keep track of calls with records that show the amount of the expense, time/place it was incurred and the business purpose.

With cell phone plans offering all sorts of deals, my suggestion is to get a separate cell phone for your business and pay $9 a month or whatever it is for your business cell line.

Wages

Do you have employees on the payroll? How about the wife and kids? Or to be politically correct, the old man and the kids? If you want to deduct wages, compensation must be ordinary and necessary as an expense for carrying on the business. It must be reasonable in amount, for personal services actually rendered, and actually paid or incurred during the tax year. Gross salaries, wages or compensation paid to relatives (including your wife or husband and kids) are deductible provided you meet the requirements that I mentioned.

Employment Credits

There are sometimes credits available to employers who hire from certain groups or certain areas of high unemployment. For more info you may want to check out IRS Publications 334 and 954.

Other Expenses

This expense category handles all ordinary and necessary business expenses not entered on other lines of Part II of our Schedule C. Items that might fit in here are bank service charges (including check printing fees, night deposit fees, etc) professional and trade dues, the cost of business related publications, laundry and cleaning of employee uniforms. All other expenses would go on Part V of the Schedule C.

Valid subscriptions for example if you were an actor or actress would be to the trade magazines or websites that have casting information if in fact it is related to the actor or actress actually getting work out of the information gleaned from their publication.

If you were an actor, dues paid to the Screen Actors Guild (SAG) could be deductible.

The Other Expenses category can be a catch all for the expenses that you aren't sure would fit in other categories. The category covers a lot of ground. Just make sure that it wouldn't fit in any other category.

Let's talk now about Home Office Expenses.

Home Office Expenses and Self Employment Taxes

Home Office Deduction

If you use part of your home for business, you may be able to deduct expenses for the business use of your home. These expenses may include mortgage interest, insurance, utilities, repairs, and depreciation. The home office deduction is available for homeowners and renters, and applies to all types of homes, from apartments to mobile homes. There are two basic requirements for your home to qualify as a deduction:

1. Regular and Exclusive Use.

You must regularly use part of your home exclusively for conducting business. For example, if you use an extra bedroom to run your online business, you can take a home office deduction for the extra bedroom.

2. Principal Place of Your Business.

You must show that you use your home as your principal place of business. If you conduct business at a location outside of your home, but also use your home substantially and regularly to conduct business, you may qualify for a home office deduction.

For example, if you have in-person meetings with patients, clients, or customers in your home in the normal course of your business, even though you also carry on business at another location, you can deduct your expenses for the part of your home used exclusively and regularly for business.

You can deduct expenses for a separate free-standing structure, such as a studio, garage, or barn, if you use it exclusively and regularly for your business. The structure does not have to be your principal place of business or the only place where you meet patients, clients, or customers.

Generally, deductions for a home office are based on the percentage of your home devoted to business use. So, if you use a whole room or part of a room for conducting your business, you need to figure out the percentage of your home devoted to your business activities.

Additional tests for employee use. If you are an employee and you use a part of your home for business, you may qualify for a deduction for its business use. You must meet the tests discussed above plus:

Your business use must be for the convenience of your employer, and you must not rent any part of your home to your employer and use the rented portion to perform services as an employee for that employer.
If the use of the home office is merely appropriate and helpful, you cannot deduct expenses for the business use of your home.

This is important if you are doing work for the same employer as both an employee and as a contractor. I have seen situations where an employer pays a salary for certain types of work and for other work generates a 1099 for the employee who is now getting treated also as a contractor by the same employer.

If the employee does sales from a home office, documentation has to be in place to show what was for the benefit for the employer and what was for the contract portion of the business income that he or she received.

Treat your work area no matter how small it is very professionally. It not only will help you at tax time but it will help you keep a business frame of mind that will help you think and work clearly for your gig.

I just cleaned my office (again) and I am able to get another couple books generated out of the situation because I can think clearer. Whoo hoo!

You get the idea.

For a full explanation of tax deductions for your home office refer to Publication 587, Business Use of Your Home. In this publication you will find:

1. The requirements for qualifying to deduct expenses for the business use of your home (including special rules for storing inventory or product samples).
2. Types of expenses you can deduct.
3. How to figure the deduction (including depreciation of your home).
4. Special rules for daycare providers.
5. Selling a home that was used partly for business.
6. Deducting expenses for furniture and equipment used in your business.
7. Records you should keep.
8. Where to deduct your expenses (including Form 8829, Expenses for Business Use of Your Home (PDF), required if you are self-employed and claiming this deduction).

Just a reminder also that the rules in the publication apply to individuals.

Make sure that your business area is used exclusively for business. The IRS is pretty serious about this and Home Office Expenses may be looked at as part of their reviews.

Self Employment Tax Calculations

First off, if you earn less than $400 in self employment income or have church employee income on a W-2 of less than $108.28 you don't need to file Schedule SE (Form 1040) Self Employment Tax.

For most of us we will have to make sure that we are paying our self employment tax.

If you go the IRS website and look for Form 1040SSE (or Self Employment Tax) you can see the form and figure your way through it. There are two flavors for filing Self Employment tax – short and long. The IRS form is pretty clear if you follow the chart on the form as to whether you need to file the short form or the long form.

The percentage for Self Employment may go up or down depending on what changes in tax law but figure that you need to comfortably put aside at least 15.3 % and then subtract half of it. So figure your share of self employment tax will be roughly 7.7%.

Estimated Tax Payments

We live in a Pay-As-You-Go tax environment and if you are earning money you should plan on paying your taxes as you earn it. When we are wage slaves, we have the money withheld by our bosses and they take care of that for us. When we are self-employed we need to handle our tax obligations quarterly.

Places to find information on quarterly payments are on the IRS website under 1040-ES (for estimated payments) and the source information can be found in Pub 505, Tax Withholding and Estimated Tax.

The nice thing about the estimated forms is that you can calculate what your tax liability will be based on the handy dandy little tax tables that are on the instructions.

Please be sure that you pick the right status (Single, Married Filing Jointly, etc) for when you are trying to determine how much you will owe in taxes.

For state taxes, you will need to find out your state's requirements. Some of them, like California, not only require quarterly payments; they require a different percentage be paid for different quarters in order to be in compliance with the state filing and reporting requirements.

****

BUSINESS FASHION TIP:

When in doubt, pay something at least for your quarterly taxes so you don't get dinged at the end of the year for higher penalties and interest. If you can't because you need the money to live on, I get it, just be aware of sticker shock at the end of the year.

****

Ready, Set, Go Sole Proprietorship, Go!

I think we've covered as much as we can. The rest now is up to you. If you have any questions, please feel free to email me kimg@kimgreenblatt.com and visit my website www.kimgreenblatt.com to see some of my other books that I have for sale.

What will make or break your business will be you. Take a look at the market that you are going to be entering in, learn all you, try to find peers you trust you can talk with and do the best planning you possibly can before you take the plunge.

Good luck and please let me know if the book helped. I am looking forward to hearing your success story!

Sincerely,

Kim

Index